W9-DGH-583

At Issue

I Is Torture Ever Justified?

Other Books in the At Issue Series:

At Issue

I Is Torture Ever Justified?

Tamara L. Roleff, Book Editor

GREENHAVEN PRESS
A part of Gale, Cengage Learning

GALE
CENGAGE Learning·

Detroit • New York • San Francisco • New Haven, Conn • Waterville, Maine • London

Christine Nasso, *Publisher*
Elizabeth Des Chenes, *Managing Editor*

© 2011 Greenhaven Press, a part of Gale, Cengage Learning.

Gale and Greenhaven Press are registered trademarks used herein under license.

For more information, contact:
Greenhaven Press
27500 Drake Rd.
Farmington Hills, MI 48331-3535
Or you can visit our Internet site at gale.cengage.com

For product information and technology assistance, contact us at

Gale Customer Support, 1-800-877-4253
For permission to use material from this text or product, submit all requests online at
www.cengage.com/permissions

Further permissions questions can be e-mailed to permissionrequest@cengage.com

Articles in Greenhaven Press anthologies are often edited for length to meet page requirements. In addition, original titles of these works are changed to clearly present the main thesis and to explicitly indicate the author's opinion. Every effort is made to ensure that Greenhaven Press accurately reflects the original intent of the authors. Every effort has been made to trace the owners of copyrighted material.

Cover Image copyright © Images.com/Corbis.

LIBRARY OF CONGRESS CATALOGING-IN-PUBLICATION DATA

Is torture ever justified? / Tamara L. Roleff, book editor.
    p. cm. -- (At issue)
    Includes bibliographical references and index.
    ISBN 978-0-7377-5091-1 (hardcover) -- ISBN 978-0-7377-5092-8 (pbk.)
    1. Torture--Juvenile literature. I. Roleff, Tamara L., 1959-
    HV8593.I8 2010
    364.6'7--dc22
                                                                        2010023162

Printed in the United States of America
1 2 3 4 5 6 7 14 13 12 11 10

Contents

Introduction

The "ticking time bomb" scenario often is cited by those who support the use of "enhanced interrogation techniques." In such a scenario, authorities are aware of a bomb that is ticking away, soon to go off, but they do not know important details, such as its location. The authorities do, however, have a suspect in custody who has information about the bomb. Supporters of the ticking time bomb scenario believe enhanced interrogation techniques are justified to obtain information from the suspect to serve the greater good—including avoiding the possibility of a massive loss of lives. Opponents of the ticking time bomb scenario argue that there are legal and moral reasons for opposing the use of enhanced interrogation techniques, which they call torture, even in a ticking time bomb situation.

While most Americans presumably have never been confronted with an actual ticking time bomb scenario, millions are familiar with the notion and are aware of the various means of torture that could be used to obtain the needed information, due to the hit television series *24*. The show stars actor Kiefer Sutherland as Jack Bauer, an agent with the fictional Counter-Terrorism Unit in Los Angeles, whose job is to prevent terrorist attacks against the United States and against numerous politicians and government administration officials. In Jane Mayer's February 19, 2007, article in the *New Yorker*, Bob Cochran, one of the creators of *24*, notes, "Most terrorism experts will tell you that the 'ticking time bomb' situation never occurs in real life, or very rarely. But on our show it happens every week."

During eight seasons of *24*, Bauer frequently used torture to obtain critical information to prevent terrorist attacks. In fact, *24* has dramatically increased the number of times torture has been shown on prime-time television. According to nonprofit organization Human Rights First, before the September 11, 2001, terrorist attacks, there were four or fewer instances of torture displayed on television each year. In 2009, there were more than 100 acts of torture depicted on television. In addition, the perpetrators of torture have changed, according to David Danzig at Human Rights First. In the same *New Yorker* article Danzig says, "It used to be almost exclusively the villains who tortured. Today, torture is often perpetrated by the heroes," despite the fact that torture is illegal under U.S. and international law.

While the show *24* is fictional, many people cite Jack Bauer and his actions as if they are real, and they use incidents from the series to support the argument that the use of torture can be justified. John Yoo, a lawyer in the U.S. Department of Justice during the George W. Bush administration and the author of the "torture memos" (official documents which delineated how far interrogators could go when questioning suspects), justifies Bauer's use of torture in his book *War by Other Means*. He says, "What if, as the Fox television program *24* recently portrayed, a high-level terrorist leader is caught who knows the location of a nuclear weapon? . . . Even Senator Charles Schumer acknowledged that, 'very few people . . . would say that torture should never, ever be used.'" Interrogators at Guantanamo Bay, Cuba, where suspected terrorists were imprisoned and questioned, were also familiar with *24* and Jack Bauer. Philippe Sands writes in his book *Torture Team* that Staff Judge Advocate Diane Beaver, an Army lawyer at Guantanamo who approved controversial interrogation techniques such as waterboarding (an interrogation method that simulates drowning), sexual humiliation, and terrorizing prisoners with dogs, said that Bauer "gave people lots of ideas." The show was immensely popular among the military personnel at the prison, she added, and a scene in which Bauer tortured a terrorist to get information about a nuclear bomb "contributed to an environment in which those at Guantanamo were encouraged to see themselves as being on the frontline."

Other fans of Bauer and his methods of obtaining information include U.S. Supreme Court Justice Antonin Scalia, who defended Bauer and his use of torture at an international legal symposium in Canada in 2007. The *Globe and Mail* reported on June 20, 2007, that during a panel discussion about international law and torture,

> A Canadian judge's passing remark—"Thankfully, security agencies in all our countries do not subscribe to the mantra, 'What would Jack Bauer do?'"—got the legal bulldog in Judge Scalia barking. The conservative jurist stuck up for Agent Bauer, arguing that fictional or not, federal agents require latitude in times of great crisis. "Jack Bauer saved Los Angeles. . . . He saved hundreds of thousands of lives," Judge Scalia said. Then, recalling Season 2, where the agent's rough interrogation tactics saved California from a terrorist nuke, the Supreme Court judge etched a line in the sand. "Are you going to convict Jack Bauer?" Judge Scalia challenged his fellow judges. "Say that criminal law is against him? 'You have the right to a jury trial?' Is any jury going to convict Jack Bauer? I don't think so. So the question is really whether we believe in these absolutes. And ought we believe in these absolutes."

According to Scalia, there are no absolutes, at least when it comes to national security. In a February 12, 2008, interview with the BBC, Scalia said the ticking time bomb scenario could justify extreme measures, "Seems to me you have to say, as unlikely as that is, it would be absurd to say that you can't stick something under the fingernails, smack them in the face. It would be absurd to say that you couldn't do that." Scalia goes on to explain that there are no easy answers, even in a ticking time bomb situation. "I certainly know you can't come in smugly and with great satisfaction and say, 'Oh, this is torture, and therefore it's no good.' You would not apply that in some real-life situations. It may not be a ticking bomb in Los Angeles, but it may be, 'Where is the group that we know is plotting this painful action against the United States? Where are they? What are they currently planning?'"

But as columnist William Bradley writes in a March 30, 2010, column on HuffingtonPost.com, "The problem with torture in the real world as a means of gaining information is not that it is immoral and never works in gaining information; it's that it's immoral and is very erratic. The problem with torture on *24* is that it always works. That's ridiculous." Concerns about torture depicted on *24* are shared by top generals in the U.S. armed forces. In Mayer's *New Yorker* article, she writes that Brigadier General Patrick Finnegan, when he was the dean of the U.S. Military Academy at West Point, met with the producers of *24* to encourage them to tone down the torture. Finnegan was concerned "that the show's central political premise—that the letter of American law must be sacrificed for the country's security—was having a toxic effect" on the cadets at the military academy, who are big fans of the show. According to Mayer, Finnegan felt "the show promoted unethical and illegal behavior and had adversely affected the training and performance of real American soldiers. 'I'd like them to stop,' he said of the show's producers. 'They should do a show where torture backfires.'" Finnegan said that *24*'s disregard for the rule of law made it increasingly more difficult to convince the cadets that torture is wrong. "The kids see it, and say, 'If torture is wrong, what about *24*?' The disturbing thing is that although torture may cause Jack Bauer some angst, it is always the patriotic thing to do."

In fact, Finnegan argued to the producers that torturing terrorists for information about a ticking time bomb is not an effective strategy. The terrorists, he said, "almost welcome torture. They expect it. They *want* to be martyred." Furthermore, he said that terrorists who know about a ticking time bomb would be even more unwilling to talk. He added, "They know if they can simply hold out several hours, all the more glory—the ticking time bomb will go off!"

Tony Lagouranis, a former Army interrogator, also tried to persuade the producers of *24* to cut back on the torture. He told Mayer that he never saw an instance when torture worked. "In Iraq, I never saw pain produce intelligence. I worked with someone who used waterboarding. I used severe hypothermia, dogs, and sleep deprivation. I saw suspects after soldiers had gone into their homes and broken their bones, or made them sit on a Humvee's hot exhaust pipes until they got third-degree burns. Nothing happened." If the suspect finally did break and give a confession, "They just told us what we already knew. It never opened up a stream of new information." In fact, he added, "Physical pain can strengthen the resolve to clam up." What works best at getting suspects to open up, Lagouranis said, is to build a sense of rapport with them. The *24* producers argue, however, that the characters do not have enough time, at least in the context of the show, to build a rapport with the suspected terrorists.

The viewpoints in *At Issue: Is Torture Ever Justified?* express some of the current thinking about the ethics, morality, and legality of torture and enhanced interrogation techniques. These arguments reveal—in stark contrast to the simplified depiction of torture in shows such as *24*—the difficulty and complexity of issues surrounding U.S. policies and definitions of torture.

1

Enhanced Interrogation Methods Are Not Justified or Necessary

Barack Obama

Barack Obama is the 44th president of the United States.

The foundations of liberty and justice in the United States are based on the U.S. Constitution, the Declaration of Independence, and the Bill of Rights. The values embodied in these documents are what make America strong and keep the country safe. Using enhanced interrogation techniques on terrorists puts these all-important values aside. Enhanced interrogation techniques are not as effective as other means of interrogation, they undermine America's laws, and they alienate the country from the rest of the world. America does not need to sacrifice its values for its security.

These are extraordinary times for our country. We're confronting a historic economic crisis. We're fighting two wars. We face a range of challenges that will define the way that Americans will live in the 21st century. So there's no shortage of work to be done, or responsibilities to bear. . . .

Keeping Americans Safe

In the midst of all these challenges, however, my single most important responsibility as President is to keep the American

Barack Obama, "Remarks by the President on National Security," May 21, 2009.

people safe. It's the first thing that I think about when I wake up in the morning. It's the last thing that I think about when I go to sleep at night.

And this responsibility is only magnified in an era when an extremist ideology threatens our people, and technology gives a handful of terrorists the potential to do us great harm. We are less than eight years removed from the deadliest attack on American soil in our history [the terrorist attacks of September 11, 2001]. We know that [terrorist organization] al Qaeda is actively planning to attack us again. We know that this threat will be with us for a long time, and that we must use all elements of our power to defeat it.

We . . . cannot keep this country safe unless we enlist the power of our most fundamental values.

Already, we've taken several steps to achieve that goal. For the first time since 2002, we're providing the necessary resources and strategic direction to take the fight to the extremists who attacked us on 9/11 in Afghanistan and Pakistan. We're investing in the 21st century military and intelligence capabilities that will allow us to stay one step ahead of a nimble enemy. We have re-energized a global non-proliferation regime to deny the world's most dangerous people access to the world's deadliest weapons. And we've launched an effort to secure all loose nuclear materials within four years. We're better protecting our border, and increasing our preparedness for any future attack or natural disaster. We're building new partnerships around the world to disrupt, dismantle, and defeat al Qaeda and its affiliates. And we have renewed American diplomacy so that we once again have the strength and standing to truly lead the world.

The Foundation of Liberty and Justice

These steps are all critical to keeping America secure. But I believe with every fiber of my being that in the long run we also cannot keep this country safe unless we enlist the power of our most fundamental values. The documents that we hold in this very hall [in the National Archives]—the Declaration of Independence, the Constitution, the Bill of Rights—these are not simply words written into aging parchment. They are the foundation of liberty and justice in this country, and a light that shines for all who seek freedom, fairness, equality, and dignity around the world.

I stand here today as someone whose own life was made possible by these documents. My father came to these shores in search of the promise that they offered. My mother made me rise before dawn to learn their truths when I lived as a child in a foreign land. My own American journey was paved by generations of citizens who gave meaning to those simple words—"to form a more perfect union." I've studied the Constitution as a student, I've taught it as a teacher, I've been bound by it as a lawyer and a legislator. I took an oath to preserve, protect, and defend the Constitution as Commander-in-Chief, and as a citizen, I know that we must never, ever, turn our back on its enduring principles for expedience sake.

I make this claim not simply as a matter of idealism. We uphold our most cherished values not only because doing so is right, but because it strengthens our country and it keeps us safe. Time and again, our values have been our best national security asset—in war and peace; in times of ease and in eras of upheaval.

Remaining True to Our Values

Fidelity to our values is the reason why the United States of America grew from a small string of colonies under the writ of an empire to the strongest nation in the world.

It's the reason why enemy soldiers have surrendered to us in battle, knowing they'd receive better treatment from America's Armed Forces than from their own government.

It's the reason why America has benefitted from strong alliances that amplified our power, and drawn a sharp, moral contrast with our adversaries.

From Europe to the Pacific, we've been the nation that has shut down torture chambers and replaced tyranny with the rule of law. That is who we are.

It's the reason why we've been able to overpower the iron fist of fascism and outlast the iron curtain of communism, and enlist free nations and free peoples everywhere in the common cause and common effort of liberty.

From Europe to the Pacific, we've been the nation that has shut down torture chambers and replaced tyranny with the rule of law. That is who we are. And where terrorists offer only the injustice of disorder and destruction, America must demonstrate that our values and our institutions are more resilient than a hateful ideology.

America Went Off Course

After 9/11, we knew that we had entered a new era—that enemies who did not abide by any law of war would present new challenges to our application of the law; that our government would need new tools to protect the American people, and that these tools would have to allow us to prevent attacks instead of simply prosecuting those who try to carry them out.

Unfortunately, faced with an uncertain threat, our government made a series of hasty decisions. I believe that many of these decisions were motivated by a sincere desire to protect the American people. But I also believe that all too often our government made decisions based on fear rather than foresight; that all too often our government trimmed facts and evidence to fit ideological predispositions. Instead of strategically applying our power and our principles, too often we set those principles aside as luxuries that we could no longer afford. And during this season of fear, too many of us—Democrats and Republicans, politicians, journalists, and citizens—fell silent.

Some have argued that brutal methods like waterboarding were necessary to keep us safe. I could not disagree more.

In other words, we went off course. And this is not my assessment alone. It was an assessment that was shared by the American people who nominated candidates for President from both major parties who, despite our many differences, called for a new approach—one that rejected torture and one that recognized the imperative of closing the prison at Guantanamo Bay [Cuba].

Now let me be clear: We are indeed at war with al Qaeda and its affiliates. We do need to update our institutions to deal with this threat. But we must do so with an abiding confidence in the rule of law and due process; in checks and balances and accountability. For reasons that I will explain, the decisions that were made over the last eight years established an ad hoc legal approach for fighting terrorism that was neither effective nor sustainable—a framework that failed to rely on our legal traditions and time-tested institutions, and that failed to use our values as a compass. And that's why I took several steps upon taking office to better protect the American people.

Enhanced Interrogation Techniques Are Banned

First, I banned the use of so-called enhanced interrogation techniques by the United States of America.

I know some have argued that brutal methods like water-boarding were necessary to keep us safe. I could not disagree more. As Commander-in-Chief, I see the intelligence. I bear the responsibility for keeping this country safe. And I categorically reject the assertion that these are the most effective means of interrogation. What's more, they undermine the rule of law. They alienate us in the world. They serve as a recruitment tool for terrorists, and increase the will of our enemies to fight us, while decreasing the will of others to work with America. They risk the lives of our troops by making it less likely that others will surrender to them in battle, and more likely that Americans will be mistreated if they are captured. In short, they did not advance our war and counterterrorism efforts—they undermined them, and that is why I ended them once and for all.

Now, I should add, the arguments against these techniques did not originate from my administration. As Senator [John] McCain once said, torture "serves as a great propaganda tool for those who recruit people to fight against us." And even under President [George W.] Bush, there was recognition among members of his own administration—including a Secretary of State, other senior officials, and many in the military and intelligence community—that those who argued for these tactics were on the wrong side of the debate, and the wrong side of history. That's why we must leave these methods where they belong—in the past. They are not who we are, and they are not America. . . .

Torture "serves as a great propaganda tool for those who recruit people to fight against us."

America Can Have Security and Values

It's no secret there is a tendency in Washington [D.C.] to spend our time pointing fingers at one another. And it's no secret that our media culture feeds the impulse that leads to a good fight and good copy. But nothing will contribute more

[to] that than an extended relitigation of the last eight years. Already, we've seen how that kind of effort only leads those in Washington to different sides, to laying blame. It can distract us from focusing our time, our efforts, and our politics on the challenges of the future.

We see that, above all, in the recent debate—how the recent debate has obscured the truth and sends people into opposite and absolutist ends. On the one side of the spectrum, there are those who make little allowance for the unique challenges posed by terrorism, and would almost never put national security over transparency. And on the other end of the spectrum, there are those who embrace a view that can be summarized in two words: "Anything goes." Their arguments suggest that the ends of fighting terrorism can be used to justify any means, and that the President should have blanket authority to do whatever he wants—provided it is a President with whom they agree.

We do not torture.

Both sides may be sincere in their views, but neither side is right. The American people are not absolutist, and they don't elect us to impose a rigid ideology on our problems. They know that we need not sacrifice our security for our values, nor sacrifice our values for our security, so long as we approach difficult questions with honesty and care and a dose of common sense. That, after all, is the unique genius of America. That's the challenge laid down by our Constitution. That has been the source of our strength through the ages. That's what makes the United States of America different as a nation.

Protecting Americans and the Rule of Law

I can stand here today, as President of the United States, and say without exception or equivocation that we do not torture, and that we will vigorously protect our people while forging a strong and durable framework that allows us to fight terrorism while abiding by the rule of law. Make no mistake: If we fail to turn the page on the approach that was taken over the past several years, then I will not be able to say that as President. And if we cannot stand for our core values, then we are not keeping faith with the documents that are enshrined in this hall.

The Framers who drafted the Constitution could not have foreseen the challenges that have unfolded over the last 222 years. But our Constitution has endured through secession and civil rights, through World War and Cold War, because it provides a foundation of principles that can be applied pragmatically; it provides a compass that can help us find our way. It hasn't always been easy. We are an imperfect people. Every now and then, there are those who think that America's safety and success requires us to walk away from the sacred principles enshrined in this building. And we hear such voices today. But over the long haul the American people have resisted that temptation. And though we've made our share of mistakes, required some course corrections, ultimately we have held fast to the principles that have been the source of our strength and a beacon to the world.

Al Qaeda Can Be Defeated

Now this generation faces a great test in the specter of terrorism. And unlike the Civil War or World War II, we can't count on a surrender ceremony to bring this journey to an end. Right now, in distant training camps and in crowded cities, there are people plotting to take American lives. That will be the case a year from now, five years from now, and—in all probability—10 years from now. Neither I nor anyone can stand here today and say that there will not be another terrorist attack that takes American lives. But I can say with certainty that my administration—along with our extraordinary troops and the patriotic men and women who defend our national security—will do everything in our power to keep the American people safe. And I do know with certainty that we can defeat al Qaeda. Because the terrorists can only succeed if they swell their ranks and alienate America from our allies, and they will never be able to do that if we stay true to who we are, if we forge tough and durable approaches to fighting terrorism that are anchored in our timeless ideals. This must be our common purpose.

I ran for President because I believe that we cannot solve the challenges of our time unless we solve them together. We will not be safe if we see national security as a wedge that divides America—it can and must be a cause that unites us as one people and as one nation. We've done so before in times that were more perilous than ours. We will do so once again.

2

Enhanced Interrogation Methods Are Legal, Justified, and Necessary

Richard B. Cheney

Richard B. Cheney served as vice president of the United States under President George W. Bush.

The United States is at war with terrorists who are seeking to destroy the country. Wars are not won by fighting defensively, and so the United States has aggressively pursued terrorists and their supporters. The key to this strategy is obtaining accurate information, and acquiring that information in time to use it. Congress and the George W. Bush Administration gave intelligence officers the tools and authority they needed to obtain vital information. Sometimes the only way to get specific information about future terrorist plans is through tough interrogations of terrorists. Enhanced interrogation techniques have saved American lives.

Being the first vice president who had also served as secretary of defense, naturally my duties tended toward national security. I focused on those challenges day to day, mostly free from the usual political distractions. . . .

The responsibilities we carried belong to others now. And though I'm not here to speak for George W. Bush, I am certain that no one wishes the current administration more suc-

Richard B. Cheney, "Remarks by Richard B. Cheney," AEI, May 21, 2009. Reproduced by permission of the American Enterprise Institute for Public Policy Research, Washington, D.C.

cess in defending the country than we do. We understand the complexities of national security decisions. We understand the pressures that confront a president and his advisers. Above all, we know what is at stake. And though administrations and policies have changed, the stakes for America have not changed. . . .

The Attack of 9/11

Our administration always faced its share of criticism, and from some quarters it was always intense. That was especially so in the later years of our term, when the dangers were as serious as ever, but the sense of general alarm after September 11, 2001 was a fading memory. Part of our responsibility, as we saw it, was not to forget the terrible harm that had been done to America . . . and not to let 9/11 become the prelude to something much bigger and far worse.

That attack itself was, of course, the most devastating strike in a series of terrorist plots carried out against Americans at home and abroad. In 1993, terrorists bombed the World Trade Center, hoping to bring down the towers with a blast from below. The attacks continued in 1995, with the bombing of U.S. facilities in Riyadh, Saudi Arabia; the killing of servicemen at Khobar Towers in 1996; the attack on our embassies in East Africa in 1998; the murder of American sailors on the USS Cole in 2000; and then the hijackings of 9/11, and all the grief and loss we suffered on that day.

We were determined to prevent attacks in the first place.

9/11 caused everyone to take a serious second look at threats that had been gathering for a while, and enemies whose plans were getting bolder and more sophisticated. Throughout the [19]90s, America had responded to these attacks, if at all, on an ad hoc basis. The first attack on the World Trade Center was treated as a law enforcement problem, with everything handled after the fact—crime scene, arrests, indictments, convictions, prison sentences, case closed.

A Policy Shift

That's how it seemed from a law enforcement perspective, at least—but for the terrorists the case was not closed. For them, it was another offensive strike in their ongoing war against the United States. And it turned their minds to even harder strikes with higher casualties. 9/11 made necessary a shift of policy, aimed at a clear strategic threat—what the Congress called "an unusual and extraordinary threat to the national security and foreign policy of the United States." From that moment forward, instead of merely preparing to round up the suspects and count up the victims after the next attack, we were determined to prevent attacks in the first place.

We could count on almost universal support back then, because everyone understood the environment we were in. We'd just been hit by a foreign enemy—leaving 3,000 Americans dead, more than we lost at Pearl Harbor. In Manhattan [New York City], we were staring at 16 acres of ashes. The Pentagon took a direct hit, and the Capitol or the White House were spared only by the Americans on Flight 93, who died bravely and defiantly.

Everyone expected a follow-on attack, and our job was to stop it. We didn't know what was coming next, but everything we did know in that autumn of 2001 looked bad. This was the world in which al-Qaeda [terrorist organization responsible for September 11, 2001, attacks] was seeking nuclear technology, and [Pakistani nuclear scientist] A.Q. Khan was selling nuclear technology on the black market. We had the anthrax attack from an unknown source. We had the training camps of Afghanistan, and dictators like Saddam Hussein with known ties to Mideast terrorists.

These are just a few of the problems we had on our hands. And foremost on our minds was the prospect of the very worst coming to pass—a 9/11 with nuclear weapons. . . .

Moving from Defense to Offense

To make certain our nation never again faced such a day of horror, we developed a comprehensive strategy, beginning with far greater homeland security to make the United States a harder target. But since wars cannot be won on the defensive, we moved decisively against the terrorists in their hideouts and sanctuaries, and committed to using every asset to take down their networks. We decided, as well, to confront the regimes that sponsored terrorists, and to go after those who provide sanctuary, funding, and weapons to enemies of the United States. We turned special attention to regimes that had the capacity to build weapons of mass destruction, and might transfer such weapons to terrorists.

The key to any strategy is accurate intelligence, and skilled professionals to get that information in time to use it.

We did all of these things, and with bipartisan support put all these policies in place. It has resulted in serious blows against enemy operations: the take-down of the A.Q. Khan network and the dismantling of Libya's nuclear program. It's required the commitment of many thousands of troops in two theaters of war, with high points and some low points in both Iraq and Afghanistan—and at every turn, the people of our military carried the heaviest burden. Well over seven years into the effort, one thing we know is that the enemy has spent most of this time on the defensive—and every attempt to strike inside the United States has failed.

So we're left to draw one of two conclusions—and here is the great dividing line in our current debate over national security. You can look at the facts and conclude that the comprehensive strategy has worked, and therefore needs to be continued as vigilantly as ever. Or you can look at the same set of facts and conclude that 9/11 was a one-off event—coordinated, devastating, but also unique and not sufficient to justify a sustained wartime effort. Whichever conclusion you arrive at, it will shape your entire view of the last seven years, and of the policies necessary to protect America for years to come.

The Need for Accurate Intelligence

The key to any strategy is accurate intelligence, and skilled professionals to get that information in time to use it. In seeking to guard this nation against the threat of catastrophic violence, our Administration gave intelligence officers the tools and lawful authority they needed to gain vital information. We didn't invent that authority. It is drawn from Article Two of the Constitution. And it was given specificity by the Congress after 9/11, in a Joint Resolution authorizing "all necessary and appropriate force" to protect the American people.

The interrogations were used on hardened terrorists after other efforts failed. They were legal, essential, justified, successful, and the right thing to do.

Our government prevented attacks and saved lives through the Terrorist Surveillance Program, which let us intercept calls and track contacts between al-Qaeda operatives and persons inside the United States. The program was top secret, and for good reason, until the editors of the *New York Times* got it and put it on the front page. After 9/11, the *Times* had spent months publishing the pictures and the stories of everyone killed by al-Qaeda on 9/11. Now here was that same newspaper publishing secrets in a way that could only help al-Qaeda. It impressed the Pulitzer committee, but it damn sure didn't serve the interests of our country, or the safety of our people.

In the years after 9/11, our government also understood that the safety of the country required collecting information known only to the worst of the terrorists. And in a few cases, that information could be gained only through tough interrogations.

In top secret meetings about enhanced interrogations, I made my own beliefs clear. I was and remain a strong proponent of our enhanced interrogation program. The interrogations were used on hardened terrorists after other efforts failed. They were legal, essential, justified, successful, and the right thing to do. The intelligence officers who questioned the terrorists can be proud of their work and proud of the results, because they prevented the violent death of thousands, if not hundreds of thousands, of innocent people.

A Differing View

Our successors in office have their own views on all of these matters.

By presidential decision, last month [April 2009] we saw the selective release of documents relating to enhanced interrogations. This is held up as a bold exercise in open government, honoring the public's right to know. We're informed, as well, that there was much agonizing over this decision.

Yet somehow, when the soul-searching was done and the veil was lifted on the policies of the Bush administration, the public was given less than half the truth. The released memos were carefully redacted to leave out references to what our government learned through the methods in question. Other memos, laying out specific terrorist plots that were averted, apparently were not even considered for release. For reasons the administration has yet to explain, they believe the public has a right to know the method of the questions, but not the content of the answers.

Political Disagreements as a Punishable Offense

Over on the left wing of the president's party, there appears to be little curiosity in finding out what was learned from the terrorists. The kind of answers they're after would be heard before a so-called "Truth Commission." Some are even demanding that those who recommended and approved the interrogations be prosecuted, in effect treating political disagreements as a punishable offense, and political opponents as criminals. It's hard to imagine a worse precedent, filled with more possibilities for trouble and abuse, than to have an incoming administration criminalize the policy decisions of its predecessors.

Apart from doing a serious injustice to intelligence operators and lawyers who deserve far better for their devoted service, the danger here is a loss of focus on national security, and what it requires. I would advise the administration to think very carefully about the course ahead. All the zeal that has been directed at interrogations is utterly misplaced. And staying on that path will only lead our government further away from its duty to protect the American people.

It is a fact that only detainees of the highest intelligence value were ever subjected to enhanced interrogation.

One person who by all accounts objected to the release of the interrogation memos was the Director of Central Intelligence, Leon Panetta. He was joined in that view by at least four of his predecessors. I assume they felt this way because they understand the importance of protecting intelligence sources, methods, and personnel. But now that this once top-secret information is out for all to see—including the enemy—let me draw your attention to some points that are routinely overlooked.

The Mastermind of 9/11

It is a fact that only detainees of the highest intelligence value were ever subjected to enhanced interrogation. You've heard endlessly about waterboarding. It happened to three terrorists. One of them was Khalid Sheikh Muhammed [KSM]—the mastermind of 9/11, who has also boasted about beheading [*Wall Street Journal* reporter] Daniel Pearl.

We had a lot of blind spots after the attacks on our country. We didn't know about al-Qaeda's plans, but Khalid Sheikh Muhammed and a few others did know. And with many thousands of innocent lives potentially in the balance, we didn't think it made sense to let the terrorists answer questions in their own good time, if they answered them at all.

Maybe you've heard that when we captured KSM, he said he would talk as soon as he got to New York City and saw his lawyer. But like many critics of interrogations, he clearly misunderstood the business at hand. American personnel were not there to commence an elaborate legal proceeding, but to extract information from him before al-Qaeda could strike again and kill more of our people.

In public discussion of these matters, there has been a strange and sometimes willful attempt to conflate what happened at Abu Ghraib prison [in Iraq] with the top secret program of enhanced interrogations. At Abu Ghraib, a few sadistic prison guards abused inmates in violation of American law, military regulations, and simple decency. For the harm they did, to Iraqi prisoners and to America's cause, they deserved and received Army justice. And it takes a deeply unfair cast of mind to equate the disgraces of Abu Ghraib with the lawful, skillful, and entirely honorable work of CIA [Central Intelligence Agency] personnel trained to deal with a few malevolent men.

Feigned Outrage and Libel

Even before the interrogation program began, and throughout its operation, it was closely reviewed to ensure that every method used was in full compliance with the Constitution, statutes, and treaty obligations. On numerous occasions, leading members of Congress, including the current speaker of the House, were briefed on the program and on the methods.

To call this a program of torture is to libel the dedicated professionals who have saved American lives, and to cast terrorists and murderers as innocent victims.

Yet for all these exacting efforts to do a hard and necessary job and to do it right, we hear from some quarters nothing but feigned outrage based on a false narrative. In my long experience in Washington, few matters have inspired so much contrived indignation and phony moralizing as the interrogation methods applied to a few captured terrorists.

I might add that people who consistently distort the truth in this way are in no position to lecture anyone about "values." Intelligence officers of the United States were not trying to rough up some terrorists simply to avenge the dead of 9/11. We know the difference in this country between justice and vengeance. Intelligence officers were not trying to get terrorists to confess to past killings; they were trying to prevent future killings. From the beginning of the program, there was only one focused and all-important purpose. We sought, and we in fact obtained, specific information on terrorist plans.

Those are the basic facts on enhanced interrogations. And to call this a program of torture is to libel the dedicated professionals who have saved American lives, and to cast terrorists and murderers as innocent victims. What's more, to completely rule out enhanced interrogation methods in the future is unwise in the extreme. It is recklessness cloaked in righteousness, and would make the American people less safe. . . .

A Request to Declassify Information

As far as the interrogations are concerned, all that remains an official secret is the information we gained as a result. Some of [President Barack Obama's] defenders say the unseen memos are inconclusive, which only raises the question why they won't let the American people decide that for themselves. I saw that information as vice president, and I reviewed some of it again at the National Archives last month [in April 2009]. I've formally asked that it be declassified so the American people can see the intelligence we obtained, the things we learned, and the consequences for national security. And as you may have heard, last week that request was formally rejected. It's worth recalling that ultimate power of declassification belongs to the President himself. President Obama has used his declassification power to reveal what happened in the interrogation of terrorists. Now let him use that same power to show Americans what did not happen, thanks to the good work of our intelligence officials.

To completely rule out enhanced interrogation methods in the future is unwise in the extreme. It is recklessness cloaked in righteousness, and would make the American people less safe.

I believe this information will confirm the value of interrogations—and I am not alone. President Obama's own Director of National Intelligence, Admiral [Dennis] Blair, has put it this way: "High value information came from interrogations in which those methods were used and provided a deeper understanding of the al-Qaeda organization that was attacking this country." End quote. Admiral Blair put that conclusion in writing, only to see it mysteriously deleted in a later version released by the administration—the missing twenty-six words that tell an inconvenient truth. But they couldn't change the words of George Tenet, the CIA Director under Presidents [Bill] Clinton and [George W.] Bush, who bluntly said: "I know that this program has saved lives. I know we've disrupted plots. I know this program alone is worth more than the FBI [Federal Bureau of Investigation], the Central Intelligence Agency, and the National Security Agency put together have been able to tell us."

If Americans do get the chance to learn what our country was spared, it'll do more than clarify the urgency and the rightness of enhanced interrogations in the years after 9/11. It may help us to stay focused on dangers that have not gone away. Instead of idly debating which political opponents to prosecute and punish, our attention will return to where it belongs—on the continuing threat of terrorist violence, and on stopping the men who are planning it. . . .

Hard Calls and High Costs

To the very end of our administration, we kept al-Qaeda terrorists busy with other problems. We focused on getting their secrets, instead of sharing ours with them. And on our watch, they never hit this country again. After the most lethal and devastating terrorist attack ever, seven and a half years without a repeat is not a record to be rebuked and scorned, much less criminalized. It is a record to be continued until the danger has passed.

Along the way there were some hard calls. No decision of national security was ever made lightly, and certainly never made in haste. As in all warfare, there have been costs—none higher than the sacrifices of those killed and wounded in our country's service. And even the most decisive victories can never take away the sorrow of losing so many of our own—all those innocent victims of 9/11, and the heroic souls who died trying to save them.

For all that we've lost in this conflict, the United States has never lost its moral bearings. And when the moral reckoning turns to the men known as high-value terrorists, I can assure you they were neither innocent nor victims. As for those who asked them questions and got answers: they did the right thing, they made our country safer, and a lot of Americans are alive today because of them.

3

Torture Is Sometimes Justified

Mirko Bagaric

Mirko Bagaric, a law professor at Deakin University in Melbourne, Australia, is the co-author, along with Julie Clarke, of Torture: When the Unthinkable Is Morally Permissible.

Every human society permits a person to kill another in self-defense without fear of legal recrimination. If it is legal to kill in self-defense, then it must be legal to inflict lesser degrees of harm, such as torture, in order to save lives. Life-saving torture sacrifices the interests of one person for the greater good. People who refuse to torture under such circumstances must take responsibility for the lives they failed to save.

The outcry by former US Vice-President Dick Cheney and [Senator] John McCain over an inquiry announced into the alleged torture tactics used by the CIA [Central Intelligence Agency] to gather information from terror suspects is the mother of double standards.

According to Cheney and McCain, the probe announced by the US Justice Department, which is aimed to cleanse the reputation of the US, will diminish the morale and effectiveness of the CIA. It could be a lot worse for the CIA. The CIA agents presumably won't be tortured during the probe to ensure that they are not holding back any information.

Demarcating the Permissible Limits of Torture

In reality the investigation is welcome. But not just because it will almost certainly result in the downfall of a "few good men". The investigation, if undertaken thoroughly, may assist in demarcating the permissible limits of torture.

In the eight years since 9/11 [2001] the US has not been subjected to a single terrorist act on its home soil. According to Cheney "the enhanced interrogation techniques were absolutely essential in saving thousands of American lives".

So was the torture justifiable? In some instances, perhaps. Contrary to prevailing sheepish sentiment, torture is permissible in extreme circumstances.

In fact advocates of a complete ban on torture don't dislike torture enough. They are willing to abdicate a potential means of preventing the torture and murder of innocent people in preference for an extremist anti-principle that "good guys never torture".

If we can kill to protect others, it is nonsense to suggest that we can't inflict lesser forms of harm, including torture, to achieve the same result.

Torture has justifiably earned a bad reputation over the centuries. It conjures up images of people being cruelly harmed for no higher ends than punishment and domination. It is not possible to mount a respectable argument that torture in such circumstances can ever be justified.

Different considerations apply when it is used for compassionate, life-saving, purposes. Every society throughout human history has accepted that it is permissible to kill in self-defence or defence of another.

If we can kill to protect others, it is nonsense to suggest that we can't inflict lesser forms of harm, including torture, to achieve the same result.

For the Greater Good

Life-saving torture has the same moral justification as other practices where we sacrifice the interests of one person for the greater good. With life-saving compassionate torture the pain inflicted on the wrongdoer is manifestly outweighed by the benefit stemming from the lives saved. The fact that wrongdoers don't expressly consent to their harsh treatment is irrelevant. Criminals and enemy soldiers don't consent to the pain inflicted on them either, yet we're not about to empty our prisons or stop shooting enemy soldiers.

The most common objection to torture is that it doesn't work. People who are tortured supposedly don't fess up accurate information. If this is right, then we should disavow torture, even as a self-defence mechanism.

Torture Has Saved Lives

But the evidence is to the contrary. There are countless instances of where torture has saved many lives. Israeli authorities claim to have foiled 90 terrorist attacks by using coercive interrogation.

Retired CIA agent John Kiriakou admitted to torturing al Qaeda [terrorist organization responsible for September 11, 2001, attacks] suspect Abu Zubaydah to obtain life-saving information. Kiriakou says the technique known as waterboarding broke Zubaydah in less than 35 seconds. The agent says he has no doubt that the information provided by Zubaydah "stopped terror attacks and saved lives".

People who would absolutely refuse to torture the bad guy to save innocent lives must take responsibility for the lives they fail to save.

The investigation into the CIA will hopefully provide a wider insight into the effectiveness of harsh interrogation techniques. If contrary to the weight of anecdotal evidence the investigation shows that those subjected to torture did not provide reliable information, then torture should be banned in all circumstances.

Time to Reconsider the Ban on Torture

But if, as is likely, torture did save thousands of lives, it is time to reconsider the legal stance on torture.

Hopefully, as a community we will never find ourselves in a position where the only way to prevent intense suffering being inflicted on innocent people is by inflicting pain on wrongdoers. Yet, the fact that the prevailing moral and legal orthodoxy supports a complete ban on torture is disturbing.

People who would absolutely refuse to torture the bad guy to save innocent lives must take responsibility for the lives they fail to save.

Wrongdoers have rights, but so too do innocent people. And the rights of the innocent can't be arbitrarily ignored simply because these individuals can't be seen or heard when we are making difficult choices.

Morality is about all humanity, and the innocent and wrongdoers are not morally equal. Fanatics who oppose torture in all cases are adopting their own form of extremism.

Kiriakou concedes that it was a tough call deciding that Zubaydah should be tortured.

But in the end he reasoned that he could not forgive himself if the CIA didn't use torture on a suspect and therefore didn't get "the nugget of information, and there was an attack".

4

Torture Is Never Justified

Becky Akers

Becky Akers is a journalist who writes frequently about security and privacy issues.

The "Ticking Time Bomb Scenario" in which a suspect is tortured for information on where the bomb is and how to defuse it, assumes that the suspect being tortured knows all the information that is needed, that he or she will divulge truthful information, and that there is time to act on the information. This is rarely the case in real life, however. Other interrogation techniques, such as gaining the suspect's trust, may require more time and patience, but they yield accurate information. Torture is and always will be wrong. It breaks the Golden Rule; it is incompatible with Christianity; it leads the torturer to other sins, such as lying and murder; and it violates the constitution.

A hidden bomb will detonate in an hour, killing hundreds of people and injuring thousands. You have the bomber in your power. Do you torture him to discover the device's location?

The Principals Committee answered "Yes" to the classic "Ticking Time Bomb Scenario." And what is the Principals Committee? A rogue group that Klingons have infiltrated aboard the starship Enterprise? A league of banana republics? No. It's part of the United States' National Security Council, and its members hail from the highest levels of the Federal

Becky Akers, "Top-Level Torture," *The New American*, vol. 24, June 9, 2008, pp. 25–29. Copyright © 2008 American Opinion Publishing Incorporated. Reproduced by permission.

government. In 2002, when it pressured the CIA [Central Intelligence Agency] to torture suspected terrorists, it included then-National Security Adviser Condoleezza Rice as its chairman as well as Vice President Dick Cheney and such former officials as Secretary of State Colin Powell, Secretary of Defense Donald Rumsfeld, CIA Director George Tenet, and Attorney General John Ashcroft.

ABC News reported on April 11, 2008 that the committee met frequently at the White House to discuss the details of torturing men—with presidential approval: "Yes, I'm aware our national security team met on this issue," George [W.] Bush acknowledged to ABC News' Martha Raddatz. "And I approved."

That approval spread like Agent Orange from the president and his advisers to the men on the ground who were guarding and interrogating prisoners. It turned Abu Ghraib's [prison in Iraq where American soldiers abused inmates] hooded, leashed, and naked "detainees" from an aberration that shamed America into official policy. No longer can the administration claim that only "a few" low-hanging "bad apples" are guilty: the president and his advisers are the biggest of those apples.

The Third Degree Approved

American governments, whether national or local, have tortured before. The armed forces flogged soldiers and sailors well into the 19th century. In 1931, the National Committee on Law Observation and Enforcement found that "the third degree—that is, the use of physical brutality, or other forms of cruelty, to obtain involuntary confessions or admissions—is widespread." But modern-day torturers have had to go underground, and they risk punishment if caught; it's been decades since torture received an official and public blessing. With two words—"I approved"—George [W.] Bush profoundly changed America.

Allegations that the United States was abusing prisoners first surfaced in 2002, but few folks noticed. Then, in April 2004, pictures from Abu Ghraib horrified the world. And so President Bush hauled out the Ticking Time Bomb Scenario to explain why a country that had proudly denounced torture was now competing with the Chinese and Soviets in barbarity. From the East Room of the White House on September 6, 2006, he claimed that there were "urgent questions" after 9/11 [2001]: "Who had attacked us? What did they want? And what else were they planning? . . . My administration . . . had to find the terrorists hiding in America and across the world, before they were able to strike our country again. So in the early days and weeks after 9/11, I directed our government's senior national security officials to do everything in their power, within our laws, to prevent another attack."

"Everything in their power" turned out to include kidnapping people suspected of terrorism and torturing them for information. The CIA and FBI [Federal Bureau of Investigation] hunted alleged terrorists overseas, shanghaied them to American military bases, and questioned them—with the president and Principals demanding answers. When answers didn't materialize quickly enough, the administration pressured agents to use what it euphemizes as "alternative interrogation techniques." The rest of us call it torture.

Alternative Interrogation Techniques

The CIA still smarts from the beating it took for its atrocities during the Vietnam War. This time it agreed to torture only if the White House explicitly authorized every slap and kick. Which is exactly what the Principals did in their meetings. In fact, their discussions were so meticulous—including the CIA's demonstrations of the torments under consideration—that "highly placed sources" described "some of the interrogation sessions" to ABC News as "almost choreographed." Nor did these conferences sicken the Principals as they reluctantly authorized desperate measures. On the contrary, those same sources quote Chairman Rice's burbling to the CIA, "This is your baby. Go do it."

The Principals mused about whether agents should punch or slap prisoners. Could they shackle them and force them to stand for hours or even days on end? What about stripping them naked in cold cells and dousing them with water? Depriving them of sleep? Torture's agony can be amplified by combining techniques: the sum is greater than the parts. So could the CIA beat a naked man while freezing him? How about strapping especially defiant suspects to a board, swaddling their mouth and nose with a towel, and flooding it with water to approximate drowning?

This last horror, known as waterboarding, is particularly effective because it combines stark panic with the physical anguish of drowning. Dr. Allen Keller, director of the Bellevue/NYU Program for Survivors of Torture, described its effects in testimony to the U.S. Senate in 2007: "As the prisoner gags and chokes, the terror of imminent death is pervasive, with all of the physiologic and psychological responses expected, including an intense stress response, manifested by . . . rapid heart beat and gasping for breath. There is a real risk of death from actually drowning or suffering a heart attack or damage to the lungs from inhalation of water. Long-term effects include panic attacks, depression and PTSD [post-traumatic stress disorder]." Victims struggle so hysterically that they sometimes snap their own bones. Waterboarding breaks prisoners in record time: most people, even "hardened terrorists," can't withstand it for longer than 30 or 40 seconds. No wonder it's beloved by some of history's most vicious regimes, including the Nazis and the Khmer Rouge.

Official Denials

And yet the [George W.] Bush administration thirsted to waterboard. Officials justified this by denying that waterboarding and their other assaults are torture. Pampered politicians who seldom suffer more than a long meeting asked us to believe that bombarding a man with rap music and blinding light while forcing him to stand in place for hours isn't torture.

"We don't engage in torture," Vice President [Dick] Cheney declared in December 2005, despite having authorized the CIA to engage in exactly that. Three months later, Chairman Rice announced, "The president made very clear from day one that he would not condone torture." Really? Then the meetings over which she presided were mutinous. Bush himself asserted on September 6, 2006, "The United States does not torture." The next month, Cheney schizophrenically insisted, "We don't torture," while admitting in the next breath that the administration authorized the waterboarding of alleged terrorist Khalid Sheik Mohammed—though Cheney dismissed nearly drowning him as "a dunk in the water." Bush again averred in October 2007, "This government does not torture people," and, in November 2007, "We do not torture." Rather, we "aggressively pursue" terrorists and "bring them to justice." Lady Justice has apparently scrapped her scales for a towel and water bucket.

Waterboarding is particularly effective because it combines stark panic with the physical anguish of drowning.

Tragically, the administration jettisoned America's honor for nothing more than a dramatic device. The Ticking Time Bomb Scenario, in which a captured terrorist knows details that will save lives but must be tortured to divulge them, first surfaced in a French novel published during the 1960s. Political philosopher Michael Walzer later speculated in an academic article about the morality—or lack thereof—of torturing under such circumstances.

Then came 9/11. Suddenly, the Scenario exploded into American thought. Attorney Alan Dershowitz announced that since torture saves lives, we should not only condone it but regulate it. In other words, we can crush a man's fingers but only after completing the proper paperwork.

A Television Show Versus Reality

Fox TV based its series *24* on a weekly ticking bomb and a silent terrorist whom hero Jack Bauer tortures into spilling his guts. Bob Cochran, one of the show's creators, told the *New Yorker*, "Most terrorism experts will tell you that the 'ticking time bomb' situation never occurs in real life, or very rarely. But on our show it happens every week." His caveat didn't keep U.S. Supreme Court Justice Antonin Scalia from publicly defending *24*'s wickedness at a conference of European and North American judges, arguing that federal agents need great leeway in trying times: "Jack Bauer saved Los Angeles. . . . He saved hundreds of thousands of lives. . . . There's a great scene where he told a guy that he was going to have his family killed. They had it on closed circuit television—and it was all staged. . . . They really didn't kill the family." Scalia seemed to imagine that Bauer's methods may be necessary to combat terrorism in real life, saying, "Is any jury going to convict Jack Bauer? I don't think so. So the question is really whether we believe in these absolutes. And ought we believe in these absolutes."

If a TV character can sway a sophisticated Supreme Court Justice, perhaps we can't blame the interrogators at Guantanamo Bay [Cuba] for looking to emulate Jack Bauer. When White House lawyers pressed Gitmo's [Guantanamo Bay] personnel for suggestions on "aggressive interrogation techniques," they copped ideas from *24*. That makes the opinion of the series' writer, Howard Gordon, foolishly optimistic: "I think people can differentiate between a television show and reality."

The Case Against Torture

The Ticking Bomb Scenario is the stuff of bestsellers because it pits a great good—saving hundreds or thousands of lives—against the horrific evil of intentionally hurting our fellow man. But when we separate it from the chills and thrills, its logic immediately falls. First, the Scenario ignores the fact that "you" aren't torturing: government is. That's the same institution that takes four days to deliver your mail across town and keeps neither bridges in Minnesota nor the dollar from collapsing. Should we entrust bureaucrats this bumbling with the awesome power to torture?

Torture seldom pries the truth from folks. Victims will say anything to stop the pain.

Second, the Scenario assumes perfect knowledge on the part of the torturer. He knows there's an actual bomb, not just the threat of one; he's sure he has the right suspect; even more improbably, he knows that his victim knows all essential facts about the bomb, especially where it is and how to defuse it. He's also certain the guy will crack under torture—not everyone does—and that he will speak truthfully about the bomb's location. If the torturer is wrong about any of these "facts," his brutality goes for naught.

Actually, torture seldom pries the truth from folks. Victims will say anything to stop the pain. Just ask Colin Powell, who still has egg on his face because he believed tales gleaned under torture. Ibn al-Shaykh al-Libi shrieked that Iraq taught al-Qaeda to use chemical and biological weapons. Powell reported this at the United Nations in 2003 and then had to recant. Another of the feds' victims, Abu Zubaida, frankly admitted he told CIA agents whatever they wanted to hear. Experts with the stomach to study such things agree that tortured confessions aren't trustworthy.

The Scenario also fails because it presents a false dichotomy: either officials torture the bomber or multitudes die. But reality is seldom that clear-cut. There are other options, and though they may require more patience and effort than waterboarding powerless prisoners, they yield accurate information. For example, the FBI works to gain a suspect's trust before questioning him. This succeeds well enough that the agency refused to cooperate with the CIA when it began torturing per presidential preference.

Torture fails in other ways, too. The country condoning it loses its soul as the unspeakable becomes ordinary and terror stalks the land. But even if torture worked, even if it alone could wring the truth from its victims without savaging society, it is still and always wrong. Under any circumstances, no matter what. There can be no debate. Those who argue otherwise leave morality, humanity, decency, and civilization far behind.

Torture inevitably leads to more sins, notably lying and murder.

Torture obviously violates the Golden Rule. We can presume that a president who brags about his Christianity should obey that divine law; unless he asks Muslims to shackle him and pour water up his nose, we can also presume that what he does unto others is not what he wants others to do unto him. Indeed, the Victim of an earlier empire's torture commanded His followers to bless—not waterboard—their enemies. One can be a torturer or a Christian but not both.

Torture inevitably leads to more sins, notably lying and murder. Bush, Cheney, Rice, et al. continue to insist that America does not torture though the CIA waterboarded at least three suspected terrorists and abused hundreds more. These politicians lie about the nature of the agonies they inflict, preposterously pretending that excruciating pain is not torture. They've lied about the accuracy and importance of the information their victims revealed; for example, they claimed that waterboarding Abu Zubaida wrung secrets from him he would have otherwise withheld. But "former FBI officials privy to details of the case continue to dispute the CIA's account of the effectiveness of the harsh measures," as the *Washington Post* noted last December [2007].

Torturers almost always murder, too—and we're not talking just "accidental" deaths from too many beatings. Hurting a man makes an implacable enemy of him, so governments often execute victims rather than free them to seek vengeance or justice.

Torture is as anti-constitutional as it is anti-Christian. It mocks everything the Founding Fathers sought to achieve, in spirit and in letter. The Constitution's entire purpose is to restrain government, to stymie its endless quest to control us, to neutralize the world's deadliest and most destructive force. Imbuing government with the virulent power of torture, then, defeats the Constitution's rationale.

Torture also specifically violates the Eighth Amendment: "Excessive bail shall not be required, nor excessive fines imposed, nor cruel and unusual punishments inflicted." Hoping to circumvent this, the administration appealed to the Department of Justice (DOJ) for advice. Attorneys Jay Bybee and John Yoo complied. In a memo dated March 14, 2003, they freed the federal government from the Eighth's constraints with facile, specious reasoning: the amendment "applies solely to those persons upon whom criminal sanctions have been imposed." It "thus has no application to those individuals who have not been punished as part of a criminal proceeding, irrespective of the fact that they have been detained by the government. . . . The detention of enemy combatants can in no sense be deemed 'punishment' for purposes of the Eighth Amendment. Unlike imprisonment pursuant to a criminal sanction, the detention of enemy combatants involves no sentence judicially imposed or legislatively required. . . . Accordingly, the Eighth Amendment has no application here."

Yoo and Bybee also redefined "torture" (torture becomes torture only when "equivalent in intensity to the pain accompanying serious physical injury, such as organ failure, impairment of bodily functions, or even death"). They capped this tour de force by shrugging that it doesn't matter anyway because national defense justifies anything; besides, the president is omnipotent in time of war. That leads to some scary stuff. Someone asked Yoo, "If the president deems that he's got to torture somebody, including by crushing the testicles of the person's child, there is no law that can stop him?" Yoo answered, "No treaty."

Torture is one of the state's favorite tools. Governments throughout history have wielded it mercilessly because pain is the simplest means of controlling people.

Yoo and Bybee's memos sailed so far over the top that even the DOJ eventually disavowed them—but not before prisoners at Abu Ghraib, Gitmo, and the CIA's secret gulags suffered agonizingly. And not before torture's evil genie escaped its bottle to haunt America.

Can we wrestle it back inside? Not easily. Torture is one of the state's favorite tools. Governments throughout history have wielded it mercilessly because pain is the simplest means of controlling people. As the United States cuts more of its constitutional moorings, as Congress continues to legislate against our interests in favor of the American empire, it will increasingly need to force compliance. And the easiest way to do that is to threaten us with severe pain. The administration has already gulled too many Americans into endorsing torture so long as the government hurts only bad guys and only to protect us. That reasoning will allow rulers to bring their tortures home, to our shores. After all, drug dealers endanger us.

So do child abusers, rapists, executives of companies that pollute or discriminate, tax resisters, political protestors, etc.

Trying to justify torture in 2005, the president blustered, "There's an enemy that lurks and plots and plans and wants to hurt America again." Sadly, it's the Bush administration.

5

Coercive Interrogation Methods Are Necessary to Protect the United States

John Yoo

John Yoo was an official in the U.S. Department of Justice from 2001 to 2003, during which time he wrote a memo authorizing and defending the use of torture on terrorists. He currently is a law professor at the University of California in Berkeley.

The civilian law-enforcement system, which was in place prior to the attacks of September 11, 2001, cannot prevent future terrorist attacks. Treating terrorists like prisoners of war, instead of like illegal combatants, gives them the same rights as accused criminals—the right to a lawyer, the right to remain silent, and the right to a speedy trial. Terrorists will use these rights to their advantage and to America's detriment. Terrorists will no longer respond to questioning, which is why coercive interrogation techniques were introduced in the first place. If terrorists are tried in a civilian court instead of a military tribunal, many will receive light sentences, because prosecutors will plea-bargain rather than compromise national security secrets in open court. Coercive interrogation techniques and military tribunals are two of the nation's most critical defenses against terrorists.

During his first week [January 2009] as commander in chief, President Barack Obama ordered the closure of

Guantanamo Bay [detention center in Cuba] and terminated the CIA's [Central Intelligence Agency] special authority to interrogate terrorists.

While these actions will certainly please his base—gone are the cries of an "imperial presidency"—they will also seriously handicap our intelligence agencies from preventing future terrorist attacks. In issuing these executive orders, Mr. Obama is returning America to the failed law enforcement approach to fighting terrorism that prevailed before Sept. 11, 2001. He's also drying up the most valuable sources of intelligence on al Qaeda [terrorist organization responsible for September 11, 2001, attacks], which, according to CIA Director Michael Hayden, has come largely out of the tough interrogation of high-level operatives during the early years of the war.

The civilian law-enforcement system cannot prevent terrorist attacks.

The question Mr. Obama should have asked right after the inaugural parade was: What will happen after we capture the next Khalid Sheikh Mohammed [KSM] or Abu Zubaydah [high-level terrorists]? Instead, he took action without a meeting of his full national security staff, and without a legal review of all the policy options available to meet the threats facing our country.

What such a review would have made clear is that the civilian law-enforcement system cannot prevent terrorist attacks. What is needed are the tools to gain vital intelligence, which is why, under President George W. Bush, the CIA could hold and interrogate high-value al Qaeda leaders. On the advice of his intelligence advisers, the president could have authorized coercive interrogation methods like those used by Israel and Great Britain in their antiterrorism campaigns. (He [Bush] could even authorize waterboarding, which he did three times in the years after 9/11.)

Changing the Rules

Mr. Obama has also ordered that all military commission trials be stayed and that the case of Ali Saleh al-Marri, the only al Qaeda operative now held on U.S. soil, be reviewed. This seems a prelude to closing the military commissions down entirely and transferring the detainees' cases to U.S. civilian courts for prosecution under ordinary criminal law. Military commission trials have been used in most American wars, and their rules and procedures are designed around the need to protect intelligence sources and methods from revelation in open court.

It's also likely Mr. Obama will declare terrorists to be prisoners of war under the Geneva Conventions. The Bush administration classified terrorists—well supported by legal and historical precedent—like pirates, illegal combatants who do not fight on behalf of a nation and refuse to obey the laws of war.

Eliminating [coercive interrogations] will mean that we will get no more information from captured al Qaeda terrorists.

The CIA must now conduct interrogations according to the rules of the Army Field Manual, which prohibits coercive techniques, threats and promises, and the good-cop bad-cop routines used in police stations throughout America. Mr. Obama has also ordered that al Qaeda leaders are to be protected from "outrages on personal dignity" and "humiliating and degrading treatment" in accord with the Geneva Conventions. His new order amounts to requiring—on penalty of prosecution—that CIA interrogators be polite. Coercive measures are unwisely banned with no exceptions, regardless of the danger confronting the country.

The Well of Information Will Dry Up

Eliminating the Bush system will mean that we will get no more information from captured al Qaeda terrorists. Every prisoner will have the right to a lawyer (which they will surely demand), the right to remain silent, and the right to a speedy trial.

The first thing any lawyer will do is tell his clients to shut up. The KSMs or Abu Zubaydahs of the future will respond to no verbal questioning or trickery—which is precisely why the Bush administration felt compelled to use more coercive measures in the first place. Our soldiers and agents in the field will have to run more risks as they must secure physical evidence at the point of capture and maintain a chain of custody that will stand up to the standards of a civilian court.

Relying on the civilian justice system not only robs us of the most effective intelligence tool to avert future attacks, it provides an opportunity for our enemies to obtain intelligence on us. If terrorists are now to be treated as ordinary criminals, their defense lawyers will insist that the government produce in open court all U.S. intelligence on their client along with the methods used by the CIA and NSA [National Security Agency] to get it. A defendant's constitutional right to demand the government's files often forces prosecutors to offer plea bargains to spies rather than risk disclosure of intelligence secrets.

Zacarias Moussaoui, the only member of the 9/11 cell arrested before the attack, turned his trial into a circus by making such demands. He was convicted after four years of pretrial wrangling only because he chose to plead guilty. Expect more of this, but with far more valuable intelligence at stake.

It is naïve to say, as Mr. Obama did in his inaugural speech, that we can "reject as false the choice between our safety and our ideals." That high-flying rhetoric means that we must give al Qaeda—a hardened enemy committed to our destruction—

the same rights as garden-variety criminals at the cost of losing critical intelligence about real, future threats.

The Nation's Defenses Are Shattered

Government policy choices are all about trade-offs, which cannot simply be wished away by rhetoric. Mr. Obama seems to have respected these realities in his hesitation to end the NSA's electronic surveillance programs, or to stop the use of predator drones to target individual al Qaeda leaders.

But in his decisions taken so precipitously just two days after the inauguration, Mr. Obama may have opened the door to further terrorist acts on U.S. soil by shattering some of the nation's most critical defenses.

6

Waterboarding Is Torture

Christopher Hitchens

Christopher Hitchens is a contributing editor for Vanity Fair *and* The Atlantic Monthly.

Waterboarding is not simulated drowning; it is controlled drowning in which the victim is brought to the edge of death and back again. The United States has prosecuted others for torture when they have been the perpetrators of waterboarding. If the United States permits its intelligence officers to waterboard terrorist suspects, it has no basis to complain if other regimes practice waterboarding on captured Americans. If the United States permits waterboarding, it becomes very difficult for it to draw the line between torture techniques that are permitted and those that are not.

Here is the most chilling way I can find of stating the matter. Until recently, "waterboarding" was something that Americans did to other Americans. It was inflicted, and endured, by those members of the Special Forces who underwent the advanced form of training known as SERE (Survival, Evasion, Resistance, Escape). In these harsh exercises, brave men and women were introduced to the sorts of barbarism that they might expect to meet at the hands of a lawless foe who disregarded the Geneva Conventions. But it was something that Americans were being trained to *resist*, not to *inflict*.

An Experiment

Exploring this narrow but deep distinction, on a gorgeous day last May [2008] I found myself deep in the hill country of western North Carolina, preparing to be surprised by a team of extremely hardened veterans who had confronted their country's enemies in highly arduous terrain all over the world. They knew about everything from unarmed combat to enhanced interrogation and, in exchange for anonymity, were going to show me as nearly as possible what real waterboarding might be like.

You feel that you are drowning because you are *drowning—or rather, being drowned, albeit slowly and under controlled conditions.*

It goes without saying that I knew I could stop the process at any time, and that when it was all over I would be released into happy daylight rather than returned to a darkened cell. But it's been well said that cowards die many times before their deaths, and it was difficult for me to completely forget the clause in the contract of indemnification that I had signed. This document (written by one who knew) stated revealingly:

> "Water boarding" is a potentially dangerous activity in which the participant can receive serious and permanent (physical, emotional and psychological) injuries and even death, including injuries and death due to the respiratory and neurological systems of the body.

As the agreement went on to say, there would be safeguards provided "during the 'water boarding' process, however, these measures may fail and even if they work properly they may not prevent [Christopher] Hitchens from experiencing serious injury or death."

Not for the Faint of Heart

On the night before the encounter I got to sleep with what I thought was creditable ease, but woke early and knew at once that I wasn't going back to any sort of doze or snooze. The first specialist I had approached with the scheme had asked my age on the telephone and when told what it was (I am 59) had laughed out loud and told me to forget it. Waterboarding is for Green Berets in training, or wiry young jihadists whose teeth can bite through the gristle of an old goat. It's not for wheezing, paunchy scribblers. For my current "handlers" I had had to produce a doctor's certificate assuring them that I did not have asthma, but I wondered whether I should tell them about the 15,000 cigarettes I had inhaled every year for the last several decades. I was feeling apprehensive, in other words, and beginning to wish I hadn't given myself so long to think about it.

I have to be opaque about exactly where I was later that day, but there came a moment when, sitting on a porch outside a remote house at the end of a winding country road, I was very gently yet firmly grabbed from behind, pulled to my feet, pinioned by my wrists (which were then cuffed to a belt), and cut off from the sunlight by having a black hood pulled over my face. I was then turned around a few times, I presume to assist in disorienting me, and led over some crunchy gravel into a darkened room. Well, mainly darkened: there were some oddly spaced bright lights that came as pinpoints through my hood. And some weird music assaulted my ears. (I'm no judge of these things, but I wouldn't have expected former Special Forces types to be so fond of New Age techno-disco.) The outside world seemed very suddenly very distant indeed.

Fear of Drowning

Arms already lost to me, I wasn't able to flail as I was pushed onto a sloping board and positioned with my head lower than my heart. (That's the main point: the angle can be slight or steep.) Then my legs were lashed together so that the board and I were one single and trussed unit. Not to bore you with my phobias, but if I don't have at least two pillows I wake up with acid reflux and mild sleep apnea, so even a merely supine position makes me uneasy. And, to tell you something I had been keeping from myself as well as from my new experimental friends, I do have a fear of drowning that comes from a bad childhood moment on the Isle of Wight, when I got out of my depth. As a boy reading the climactic torture scene of *1984*, where what is in Room 101 is the worst thing in the world, I realize that somewhere in my version of that hideous chamber comes the moment when the wave washes over me. Not that that makes me special: I don't know anyone who *likes* the idea of drowning. As mammals we may have originated in the ocean, but water has many ways of reminding us that when we are in it we are out of our element. In brief, when it comes to breathing, give me good old air every time.

You may have read by now the official lie about this treatment, which is that it "simulates" the feeling of drowning. This is not the case. You feel that you are drowning because you *are* drowning—or, rather, being drowned, albeit slowly and under controlled conditions and at the mercy (or otherwise) of those who are applying the pressure. The "board" is the instrument, *not* the method. You are not being boarded. You are being watered. This was very rapidly brought home to me when, on top of the hood, which still admitted a few flashes of random and worrying strobe light to my vision, three layers of enveloping towel were added. In this pregnant darkness, head downward, I waited for a while until I abruptly felt a slow cascade of water going up my nose. Determined to resist if only for the honor of my navy ancestors who had so often been in peril on the sea, I held my breath for a while and then had to exhale and—as you might expect—inhale in turn. The inhalation brought the damp cloths tight against my

55

nostrils, as if a huge, wet paw had been suddenly and annihilatingly clamped over my face. Unable to determine whether I was breathing in or out, and flooded more with sheer panic than with mere water, I triggered the pre-arranged signal and felt the unbelievable relief of being pulled upright and having the soaking and stifling layers pulled off me. I find I don't want to tell you how little time I lasted.

If waterboarding does not constitute torture, then there is no such thing as torture.

Waterboarding Is Torture

This is because I had read that Khalid Sheikh Mohammed, invariably referred to as the "mastermind" of the atrocities of September 11, 2001, had impressed his interrogators by holding out for upwards of two minutes before cracking. (By the way, this story is not confirmed. My North Carolina friends jeered at it. "Hell," said one, "from what I heard they only washed his damn face before he babbled.") But, hell, I thought in my turn, no Hitchens is going to do worse than *that*. Well, O.K., I admit I didn't outdo him. And so then I said, with slightly more bravado than was justified, that I'd like to try it one more time. There was a paramedic present who checked my racing pulse and warned me about adrenaline rush. An interval was ordered, and then I felt the mask come down again. Steeling myself to remember what it had been like last time, and to learn from the previous panic attack, I fought down the first, and some of the second, wave of nausea and terror but soon found that I was an abject prisoner of my gag reflex. The interrogators would hardly have had time to ask me any questions, and I knew that I would quite readily have agreed to supply any answer. I still feel ashamed when I think about it. Also, in case it's of interest, I have since woken up trying to push the bedcovers off my face, and if I do anything that makes me short of breath I find myself clawing at the air with a horrible sensation of smothering and claustrophobia. No doubt this will pass. As if detecting my misery and shame, one of my interrogators comfortingly said, "Any time is a long time when you're breathing water." I could have hugged him for saying so, and just then I was hit with a ghastly sense of the sadomasochistic dimension that underlies the relationship between the torturer and the tortured. I apply the Abraham Lincoln test for moral casuistry: "If slavery is not wrong, nothing is wrong." Well, then, if waterboarding does not constitute torture, then there is no such thing as torture.

If we allow it and justify it, we cannot complain if it is employed in the future by other regimes on captive U.S. citizens.

The Language of Torture

I am somewhat proud of my ability to "keep my head," as the saying goes, and to maintain presence of mind under trying circumstances. I was completely convinced that, when the water pressure had become intolerable, I had firmly uttered the predetermined code word that would cause it to cease. But my interrogator told me that, rather to his surprise, I had not spoken a word. I had activated the "dead man's handle" that signaled the onset of unconsciousness. So now I have to wonder about the role of false memory and delusion. What I do recall clearly, though, is a hard finger feeling for my solar plexus as the water was being poured. What was that for? "That's to find out if you are trying to cheat, and timing your breathing to the doses. If you try that, we can outsmart you. We have all kinds of enhancements." I was briefly embarrassed that I hadn't earned or warranted these refinements, but it hit me yet again that this is certainly the *language* of torture.

Maybe I am being premature in phrasing it thus. Among the veterans there are at least two views on all this, which means in practice that there are two opinions on whether or not "waterboarding" constitutes torture. I have had some extremely serious conversations on the topic, with two groups of highly decent and serious men, and I think that both cases have to be stated at their strongest.

It may be a means of extracting information, but it is also a means of extracting junk information.

The Case Against Waterboarding as Torture

The team who agreed to give me a hard time in the woods of North Carolina belong to a highly honorable group. This group regards itself as out on the front line in defense of a society that is too spoiled and too ungrateful to appreciate those solid, underpaid volunteers who guard us while we sleep. These heroes stay on the ramparts at all hours and in all weather, and if they make a mistake they may be arraigned in order to scratch some domestic political itch. Faced with appalling enemies who make horror videos of torture and beheadings, they feel that they are the ones who confront denunciation in our press, and possible prosecution. As they have just tried to demonstrate to me, a man who has been waterboarded may well emerge from the experience a bit shaky, but he is in a mood to surrender the relevant information and is unmarked and undamaged and indeed ready for another bout in quite a short time. When contrasted to actual torture, waterboarding is more like foreplay. No thumbscrew, no pincers, no electrodes, no rack. Can one say this of those who have been captured by the tormentors and murderers of (say) Daniel Pearl [a *Wall Street Journal* reporter who was kidnapped and killed in Pakistan]? On this analysis, any call to indict the United States for torture is therefore a lame and diseased attempt to arrive at a moral equivalence between those who defend civilization and those who exploit its freedoms to hollow it out, and ultimately to bring it down. I myself do not trust anybody who does not clearly understand this viewpoint.

The Case for Waterboarding as Torture

Against it, however, I call as my main witness Mr. Malcolm Nance. Mr. Nance is not what you call a bleeding heart. In fact, speaking of the coronary area, he has said that, in battlefield conditions, he "would personally cut [Osama] bin Laden's [leader of al Qaeda] heart out with a plastic M.R.E. [Meal, Ready to Eat] spoon." He was to the fore on September 11, 2001, dealing with the burning nightmare in the debris of the Pentagon. He has been involved with the SERE program since 1997. He speaks Arabic and has been on al-Qaeda's tail since the early 1990s. His most recent book, *The Terrorists of Iraq*, is a highly potent analysis both of the jihadist threat in Mesopotamia and of the ways in which we have made its life easier. I passed one of the most dramatic evenings of my life listening to his cold but enraged denunciation of the adoption of waterboarding by the United States. The argument goes like this:

1. Waterboarding is a deliberate torture technique and has been prosecuted as such by our judicial arm when perpetrated by others.

2. If we allow it and justify it, we cannot complain if it is employed in the future by other regimes on captive U.S. citizens. It is a method of putting American prisoners in harm's way.

3. It may be a means of extracting information, but it is also a means of extracting junk information. (Mr. Nance told me that he had heard of someone's being com-

pelled to confess that he was a hermaphrodite. I later had an awful twinge while wondering if I myself could have been "dunked" this far.) To put it briefly, even the C.I.A. [Central Intelligence Agency] sources for the *Washington Post* story on waterboarding conceded that the information they got out of Khalid Sheikh Mohammed was "not all of it reliable." Just put a pencil line under that last phrase, or commit it to memory.

4. It opens a door that cannot be closed. Once you have posed the notorious "ticking bomb" question, and once you assume that you are in the right, what will you *not* do? Waterboarding not getting results fast enough? The terrorist's clock still ticking? Well, then, bring on the thumbscrews and the pincers and the electrodes and the rack.

A SERE School for Terrorists

Masked by these arguments, there lurks another very penetrating point. Nance doubts very much that Khalid Sheikh Mohammed lasted that long under the water treatment (and I am pathetically pleased to hear it). It's also quite thinkable, *if* he did, that he was trying to attain martyrdom at our hands. But even if he endured so long, and since the United States has in any case bragged that *in fact* he did, one of our worst enemies has now become one of the founders of something that will someday disturb your sleep as well as mine. To quote Nance:

> Torture advocates hide behind the argument that an open discussion about specific American interrogation techniques will aid the enemy. Yet, convicted Al Qaeda members and innocent captives who were released to their host nations have already debriefed the world through hundreds of interviews, movies and documentaries on exactly what methods they were subjected to and how they endured. Our own

missteps have created a cadre of highly experienced lecturers for Al Qaeda's own virtual SERE school for terrorists.

Making Lies into Truths

Which returns us to my starting point, about the distinction between training *for* something and training to resist it. One used to be told—and surely with truth—that the lethal fanatics of al-Qaeda were schooled to lie, and instructed to claim that they had been tortured and maltreated whether they had been tortured and maltreated or not. Did we notice what a frontier we had crossed when we admitted and even proclaimed that their stories might in fact be true? I had only a very slight encounter on that frontier, but I still wish that my experience were the only way in which the words "waterboard" and "American" could be mentioned in the same (gasping and sobbing) breath.

7

Waterboarding Is Not Torture

Andrew C. McCarthy

Andrew C. McCarthy, a columnist for National Review *maga-zine, is a former assistant U.S. attorney who prosecuted Sheik Omar Abdel Rahman and eleven others for the 1993 World Trade Center bombing.*

While U.S. Attorney General Eric Holder has claimed that water-boarding is torture, even he admitted, in Congressional testi-mony, that it is the interrogator's intent that determines whether or not a particular technique is torture. Legal statutes indicate that, if an interrogator does not intend to permanently harm the suspect, and if no permanent harm is done, then the interroga-tion method is not torture. The Central Intelligence Agncey (CIA) interrogators who use waterboarding to get information have no intent to torture, and therefore, waterboarding is not torture.

There was a little noticed bombshell in Washington's [D.C.] waterboarding melodrama last week [in May 2009]. And it wasn't [speaker of the House of Representatives] Nancy Pelosi's implosion in a Capitol Hill press room, where she yet again tried to explain her inexplicable failure to protest the CIA's [Central Intelligence Agency] "torturing" of detainees. No, this one detonated in the hearing room of the House Ju-diciary Committee. There, Attorney General Eric Holder inad-vertently destroyed the warped basis for his claim that water-boarding, as administered by the CIA, amounted to torture.

Andrew C. McCarthy, "On 'Torture,' Holder Undoes Holder," *National Review Online*, May 19, 2009. Copyright © 2009 by National Review, Inc., 215 Lexington Avenue, New York, NY 10016. Reproduced by permission.

As originally reported by Connie Hair of *Human Events,* Holder's undoing was the result of deft questioning by two committee Republicans: Dan Lungren, California's former state attorney general, and Louie Gohmert, the former chief judge of a Texas appeals court. The two congressmen highlighted a fatal flaw in Holder's theory. Moreover, they demonstrated that—despite having accused the CIA and the [President George W.] Bush administration of war crimes by cavalierly branding waterboarding as torture—the attorney general has still not acquainted himself with the legal elements of a torture offense, particularly the required mental state. This is remarkable, given that Holder's own department explained these elements less than a month ago in a federal appeals court brief.

Intent Is Key

Rep. Lungren pointed out that if the attorney general truly believes "waterboarding is torture," he must also think we torture our own Navy SEALs and other special-operations personnel when we waterboard them as part of their training. "No . . . not in the legal sense," countered Holder. You see, said he, it's "a fundamentally different thing," because

> we're doing something for training purposes to try to equip them with the tools to, perhaps, resist torture techniques that might be used on them. There is not the intent to do that which is defined as torture—which is to inflict serious bodily or mental harm. It's for training. It's different.

What removes an act from the ambit of torture (besides lack of severe pain) is intent.

But it's not different because "it's for training." Look at the torture statute (Sections 2340 and 2340A of the federal penal code) and try to find a "training" exception. There isn't one. What removes an act from the ambit of torture (besides lack of severe pain) is *intent*. Lungren pressed this point, and Holder admitted that the training was "not torture in the legal sense because we're not doing it with the intention of harming these people physically or mentally." *Intent*, he acknowledged, was the key question.

Then, Lungren pounced. The CIA interrogators who questioned top al-Qaeda captives like Khalid Sheikh Mohammed and Abu Zubaydah intended no more harm to them than Navy instructors intended to their SEAL trainees. In fact, we know that the CIA went to great lengths, under Justice Department guidance, precisely to avoid severe harm. Their purpose, Rep. Lungren observed, was to "solicit information," not to inflict torture.

Holder was trapped. He responded with some blather about how "when the Communist Chinese did [waterboarding], when the Japanese did it, when they did it in the Spanish Inquisition, we knew then that that was not a training exercise they were engaging in. They were doing it in a way that is violative of . . . all the statutes that recognize what torture is."

Let's put aside that it's unlikely the Spanish Inquisition had a torture statute—after all, the United States managed to get along without one until 1994. Let's even ignore the fact that the regimes Holder cited are not known to have rigorously limited their practitioners to no more than six applications of water (none longer than 40 seconds long) during any interrogation session (none longer than two hours long) on any day (during which there could be no more than two sessions) in any month (during which there could be no more than five days on which waterboarding occurred). Let's just stick with intent. Holder's exemplars involve the sadistic, programmatic infliction of severe, lasting, and often lethal pain— "water treatment" nowhere near as benign as the CIA's, frequently coupled with atrocities like beating, rape, burning, and other unspeakable abuses. The practices of those regimes were designed exactly to torture, whether out of vengeance, the desire to intimidate a population, or the coercion of false confessions for show-trials—not to collect true, life-saving intelligence for the protection of civilian populations.

Ill-Informed About the Law

When Rep. Gohmert followed up on the issue of intent, it became starkly apparent that our attorney general is either badly ill-informed about the law, or simply willing to misstate it. Gohmert asked: "If our officers, when waterboarding, had no intent to do permanent harm and, in fact, knew absolutely they would do no permanent harm to the person being waterboarded, and their only intent was to get information to save people in this country, then they would not have tortured, under your definition. Isn't that correct?"

Holder summarily rejected this assessment, lamely attempting to fend it off by saying it would depend "on the intention of the person." But of course, Gohmert had already stated the intention, very exactingly, in his hypothetical. In a corner again, Holder blundered. Whether Gohmert's example would constitute torture, he surmised, suddenly depended not so much on the intention of the officers but on whether their act (i.e., waterboarding) would have the "logical . . . result" of "physically or mentally harm[ing] the person."

Torture . . . is not a general-intent crime. It calls for proof of specific *intent.*

Gohmert demurred, asserting: If "someone has to believe that they are doing harm to someone in order to . . . torture, then if . . . you knew without any question there was no harm being done, then there's no torture."

Holder replied,

No, I wouldn't say that. . . . You can delude yourself into thinking that "what I'm doing is not causing any physical harm, it's not causing any mental harm," and somebody, a neutral trier of fact ... could look at that and make the determination that, in spite of what you said, that what you have indicated is not consistent with the facts, not consistent with your actions, and therefore you're liable under the statute for the harm that you caused.

General Versus Specific Intent

That is completely wrong. What Holder described is the legal concept of a "general intent" crime. Most crimes fall into this category. To find guilt, all the jury (the "neutral trier of fact") has to determine is (a) that you knew what you were doing (i.e., you intended to shoot the gun or rob the bank—you didn't do it by mistake), and (b) the result was the logical outcome that anyone who performed such an act should have expected.

If his motive was not to torture, it is not torture.

Torture, however, is not a general-intent crime. It calls for proof of *specific* intent. . . . The Third Circuit U.S. Court of Appeals explained the difference in its *Pierre* [*v. Attorney General*] case last year to establish torture, it must be proved that the accused torturer had "the motive or purpose" to commit torture. Sharpening the distinction, the judges used an example from a prior torture case—an example that thoroughly refutes Holder's attempt to downgrade torture to a general-intent offense: "The mere fact that the Haitian authorities have knowledge that severe pain and suffering may result by placing detainees in these conditions does not support a finding that the Haitian authorities intend to inflict severe pain and suffering. The difference goes to the heart of the distinction between general and specific intent."

To state the matter plainly, the CIA interrogators did not inflict severe pain and had no intention of doing so. The law of the United States holds that, even where an actor *does* inflict severe pain, there is still no torture unless it was his objective to do so. It doesn't matter what the average person might think the "logical" result of the action would be; it matters what specifically was in the mind of the alleged torturer—if his motive was not to torture, it is not torture.

Waterboarding . . . cannot be torture because there is no intention to inflict severe mental or physical pain.

One might have expected Holder to know that. The argument was used in a DOJ [Department of Justice] filing before the Sixth Circuit U.S. Court of Appeals only three weeks ago. Indeed, the Haitian example cited by the Third Circuit is quoted here, word-for-word, from the brief filed by Holder's own department.

The Bottom Line

The bottom line is, Rep. Lungren skillfully steered Attorney General Holder into the truth: As a matter of law, CIA waterboarding—like the same waterboarding actions featured in Navy SEALs training—cannot be torture because there is no intention to inflict severe mental or physical pain; the exercise is done for a different purpose. When Rep. Gohmert's questioning made it crystal clear that Holder's simplistic "waterboarding is torture" pronouncement was wrong, the attorney general—rather than admitting error—tried to change the legal definition of torture in a manner that contradicted a position the Justice Department had just urged on the federal courts. It seems that, for this attorney general, there is one torture standard for Bush administration officials, and another one for everybody else.

Good to see Holder has ended all that unseemly politicizing of the Justice Department.

8

It Is Difficult to Know What Is Torture and What Is Not

Andrew Coyne

Andrew Coyne is the national editor for Maclean's, *a weekly news magazine in Canada.*

Torture is a complex issue. The issue is not whether torture is effective or justified, but how torture is defined. It is difficult to draw a line between what is discomfort and what is abuse. But even if an act is not torture, commission of that act is not necessarily right; it can still be cruel and degrading treatment.

Torture, like terrorism, is an issue that does not admit easily of complexity. The same people who mocked [President] George W. Bush for his "black and white" thinking on terrorism ("you are either with us or you are with the terrorists") stand ready to accuse anyone who confesses any uncertainty about the issue—what tactics may be permitted in interrogating terrorist suspects, whether the CIA's [Central Intelligence Agency] treatment of detainees crossed the line, whether to prosecute those who did—of "defending torture."

At the same time, any attempt to impose legal limits on the war on terror, to hold to account those who may have broken the law in the prosecution of their duties, invites equally lurid accusations from the other side—of criminalizing policy differences, of demoralizing the CIA, even of aiding the terrorists. So it is a probable testament to the political independence, if not the political judgment, of the U.S. attorney general, Eric Holder, that he was willing to wade into this swamp. His boss may come to wish he hadn't.

It is a fundamental tenet of law that those accused of crimes must be possessed of 'the guilty mind'—it must be shown they knew they were breaking the law, or at the very least should have known.

Holder's decision last week [in September 2009] to launch an inquiry, headed by special prosecutor John Durham, into allegations of CIA abuse of detainees under the [George W.] Bush administration, has already drawn fire from both the left and right. Critics among human rights groups and Democratic activists are upset that the investigation will be confined to cases where interrogators went beyond the guidelines set down by White House lawyers in the Office of Legal Counsel—the infamous "torture memos"—and not to the lawyers themselves, or even their political masters. Meanwhile, critics to Holder's right—notably the former vice-president, Dick Cheney, but also some Democrats—denounce the investigation as at best superfluous, at worst a partisan witch hunt.

A "Guilty Mind" Is Needed for Prosecution

But it's hard to see what alternative Holder had. It is a fundamental tenet of law that those accused of crimes must be possessed of "the guilty mind"—it must be shown they knew they were breaking the law, or at the very least should have known. You can't prosecute interrogators for following expert legal advice, and you can't prosecute lawyers for offering it, however flawed it might have been. You can, however, prosecute where interrogators deliberately ignored or exceeded the guidelines—as a 2004 report by the CIA inspector general, also released last week, suggests—in violation of the statutory ban on inflicting "severe physical or mental pain or suffering." And you can prosecute where a lawyer knowingly counsels actions that are against the law. But that's a much harder thing to prove.

Indeed, it is a legitimate criticism of Holder that the cases of alleged detainee abuse most likely to come under scrutiny had earlier been referred to a task force of Justice Department prosecutors, admittedly under the previous administration. In all but one case they declined to prosecute, citing insufficient evidence. But nothing says their judgment cannot be reviewed, and in the fevered political climate surrounding the issue, there is something to be said for a little bipartisan redundancy. No, you don't want each incoming administration investigating the last, or prosecuting those who acted in good faith on the basis of different beliefs, in this case about how best to defend the country. But neither is it plausible to think that such an emotive debate could just be left to lie, notwithstanding [President] Barack Obama's professed desire to "look forward, not backward." If Durham reports, as he likely will, that he sees no grounds for prosecution, that is more likely to put the issue to rest.

It would seem hard to explain, if torture is so ineffective at extracting information, why it is also so widespread.

That will disappoint those for whom the issue boils down to a simple catechism: torture is against the law. The Bush administration tortured. People who break the law should be punished. It will equally disappoint those enamoured of an even simpler catechism: torture works. Whatever works in the fight against terrorism is justified. Nothing should be allowed to detract from that task. Cheney himself defended the policy last weekend as "absolutely essential."

A Yearning for Moral Clarity

Both sides yearn for moral clarity, which is understandable and indeed desirable. But clarity is not achieved by reductionism. It is comforting, on the one hand, to believe that "torture never works"—that, as it is often said, prisoners under torture will say anything to put an end to their suffering. But it bumps up against the uncomfortable fact that in some cases there is evidence that it does work. The *Washington Post* reported over the weekend [in September 2009] that waterboarding—the harshest method used by the CIA, and the one most widely agreed to meet the definition of torture, though it was applied to only three subjects—was responsible for turning Khalid Sheik Mohammed, the mastermind of Sept. 11, into the CIA's "preeminent source" on al-Qaeda. The source? The same 2004 inspector general's report that prompted Holder's inquiry.

Indeed, it would seem hard to explain, if torture is so ineffective at extracting information, why it is also so widespread. Possibly prisoners will say anything, including the truth.

The Efficacy of Torture

On the other hand, even if they are induced to give up true information in some cases, how is it to be known whether they are telling the truth in any given case? (In fact, Mohammed told the Red Cross that much of what he told the CIA was untrue.) Or suppose they are. Is that enough to justify it? Is there not still some weighing required? Does the value of the information obtained outweigh the harm done—to the prisoner, to our own consciences? Could the same information not have been obtained by other, less repugnant ways? And of course, there is the little matter that, whether it works or not, torture is against the law.

Merely debating the efficacy of torture, in other words, does not get us very far—but neither does debating its morality, without regard to efficacy. The philosophy class example, of the prisoner with foreknowledge of a "ticking bomb" that will kill thousands, shows the weakness of both approaches. It requires a certain kind of moral obtuseness to insist that no use of torture could ever be justified, even where it would save thousands of lives. But is such a neat example ever likely to come up in the real world, and if it did, how could you know with certainty that your prisoner was it? You might have the wrong guy. He might not tell you anything. You might be too late. (Of course, there's another sense in which it's an academic question. No court would convict an intelligence agent whose actions saved thousands of lives, whatever the law may say.)

Defining Torture

But is torture, itself, the issue? The question, for the most part, is not whether torture is justified, but how it is defined. The "torture memos," despite the name, were in fact intended to define what was permissible under the law. Whether White House lawyers succeeded in drawing the line correctly, legally or morally, does not mean that no line need be drawn. Yet that is the unspoken premise of much commentary on the issue. All kinds of harsh tactics get lumped together as torture, from the merely unpleasant to the clearly appalling. Among the "abusive" practices listed in press accounts have been the provision of unappetizing food, or the use of female interrogators.

But the principle cannot be that interrogation subjects should be subjected to no discomfort or duress whatever. The very act of interrogating someone is highly stressful, implicitly coercive. As, for that matter, is imprisonment. The U.S. Army field manual's rules on interrogation, while expressly forbidding many of the practices authorized under the Bush administration, also allows for tactics designed to disorient, confuse or demoralize the prisoner. Among the 18 listed "approach techniques," for example, is the "emotional fear-up" approach, in which the interrogator "identifies . . . or creates" a fear in the subject, then links its elimination to his co-operation. The interrogator "must be extremely careful that he does not threaten or coerce" the subject. Still, he can make vaguely ominous statements such as, "you know what can happen to you here?"

Where to Draw the Line

What that ought to suggest is that it is not always obvious where the line is to be drawn, between a fear and a threat, between discomfort and abuse. How long can a prisoner be deprived of sleep, for example, before it becomes torture? Two days? Four? 11? The army field manual says a prisoner must be given at least four hours of continuous sleep every 24 hours. Is anything less than that torture?

Merely because something does not count as torture does not make it right.

One is acutely aware, in raising such concerns, of the slippery slope that beckons. "This is how it starts," you think. You begin by making these nice distinctions and you end up justifying concentration camps. But this is also how it starts: by failing to make elementary moral distinctions. By treating every evil as if it were equivalent. We do have to draw lines. But we have to draw them with clear heads.

Of course, merely because something does not count as torture does not make it right. A practice may still be denounced as cruel and degrading even if it does not meet the strict legal definition of torture. It may be, as [Canadian politician] Michael Ignatieff has argued, that we should insist on prohibiting both, to give ourselves a moral buffer zone, as it were, a margin for error around the hard core of the clearly abhorrent. But that still does not relieve us of the responsibility of asking where that line should be drawn.

It may be that we will decide that some techniques which we would not otherwise countenance might be permissible, in view of the unique threat posed by modern macroterrorism. It was also Michael Ignatieff, after all, who suggested some forms of "coercive interrogation" or duress might be permissible—mild sleep deprivation, say—while continuing to outlaw any "physical coercion or abuse." For this he has been called an apologist for torture. Presumably, in due course, so will Holder.

9

Torture Takes Many Forms

Becky Akers

Becky Akers writes frequently about issues related to privacy and security. Her writing has been published in American History Magazine, *the* New York Post, *the* Christian Science Monitor, *and others.*

Becky Akers reviews Standard Operating Procedure, *a book that exposes the military's use of torture by quoting prison personnel. American soldiers, stationed at Abu Ghraib prison in Iraq, detail the torture inflicted upon prisoners. The torture ranged from putting prisoners in garbage cans filled with ice water, to parading them naked while terrorizing them with dogs. Although physical and emotional torture is supposed to force intelligence out of prisoners, the information extracted is mostly unreliable.*

"You had stress positions," recalls one of the soldiers guarding the prisoners, "and you escalated the stress positions. Forced to stand for hours at a time . . . hold bottles of water out to [their] sides . . . handcuffs behind their backs, high up, in very uncomfortable positions, or chained down. . . . Then you had the submersion. You put the people in garbage cans, and you'd put ice in it, and water. Or stick them underneath the shower spigot naked, and open a window while it was like forty degrees outside, and watch them disappear into themselves before they go into shock."

You might guess this testimony comes from Communist China or Cuba. But the speaker is an American soldier sta-

Becky Akers, "When Torture Becomes Standard: *Standard Operating Procedure* Exposes the Military's Use of Torture by Quoting Verbatim from Prison Personnel Stationed at Abu Ghraib," *New American*, July 21, 2008. Reproduced by permission.

tioned at the prison camp in Abu Ghraib, Iraq. Authors Philip Gourevitch and Errol Morris draw much of *Standard Operating Procedure* verbatim from interviews with the prison's personnel. These detail the sexual humiliation and nudity that were common there. Male and female soldiers regularly stripped prisoners, then dressed them in women's panties or paraded them naked while terrorizing them with dogs. Both tortures are diabolical: canines and carnality are taboo in Arab culture.

At least one prisoner died from the abuse. Since the Army didn't admit to his murder, let alone investigate it, no one knows exactly why he died.

The Different Forms of Torture

Depriving prisoners of sleep was just as common. Indeed, this torment introduced inmates to Abu Ghraib's horrors: "'We just had [a new prisoner] out and PT'd him the whole night,' [another guard, Charles] Graner said, and by PT he meant everything from deep knee bends to low crawling naked up and down the tier," so that the front of the body scraped along the concrete floor. When the guards tired of watching naked men bleed, they pressed boxes of rations into duty. "MRE [Meal, Ready to Eat] cartons were always handy: a prisoner could be made to stand still until he fell off, or to hold one out in front of him until its weight became unbearable. And whatever the drill was, he'd be yelled at. In a full-on PT session, he might get shoved or slapped around, too."

At least one prisoner died from the abuse. Since the Army didn't admit to his murder, let alone investigate it, no one knows exactly why he died. Or when: neither the interrogator questioning him nor the guards shackling him in "stress positions" could figure out why their victim wasn't screaming with pain. They eventually realized he was dead.

Torture Doesn't Work

Supposedly, this physical and emotional torture would wring intelligence from prisoners. Two factors made this impossible.

First, at least 75 percent of Abu Ghraib's inmates were innocent of everything but being in the wrong place at the wrong time, as even the U.S. military finally admitted. The Army routinely retaliates when Iraqi insurgents strike it by sweeping up everyone within the vicinity; it's as though the cops from your local precinct arrested everyone on your block because someone blew up their cruiser. Iraqis who live, work, or happen to be driving down the street when a bomb explodes are no guiltier than you, but American soldiers "detain" them nonetheless, usually without charges or even the promise of a trial. The remaining quarter of Abu Ghraib's prisoners, while "criminal," were so designated by Iraqi justice, such as it is. Even if an alleged rapist is truly guilty, he probably doesn't know much about terrorists' plans against the American invaders.

Among the excuses for Abu Ghraib's excesses is that low-ranking, untrained soldiers ran it without supervision.

Second, torture doesn't extract reliable intelligence. *Standard Operating Procedure* quotes Tim Dugan, "a civilian interrogator" on contract to the Army who was assigned to Abu Ghraib. He shows a professional's contempt for its crudity and cruelty: "The thought of abusing detainees—don't have to abuse the detainees. I'm an interrogator. . . . For years, I found out what my Christmas presents were before Christmas just by asking open-ended leading questions. Eighty percent of the population, you can walk up and talk to them, and they'll tell you everything. One of the things an interrogator does every time is evaluate the truthfulness and reliability of the information given. That's the very last paragraph of every report you ever write. So, if I get information through torture, I have no way to verify anything. . . . You're going to tell me whatever the hell you want so the pain stops."

The abyss between actual interrogation and Abu Ghraib's sick parody of it stands stark in Dugan's description of "pocket litter"—a concept foreign to everyone at the prison. "Pocket litter," Dugan explains, "is whatever the guy was arrested with, whatever he had in his pockets, on his person. Did he have a gun? Did he have a bloody rag? If he says he wasn't shooting mortars, and he has a mortar table in his pocket litter, then he was probably shooting frickin' mortars. That's evidence." We might hope the Army would have enough wits to capitalize on Dugan's skills even if it couldn't emulate them, but no. "Within an hour" of his arrival at Abu Ghraib, officers transferred him to neutralize the threat that so knowledgeable a witness posed.

The suffering U.S. troops have inflicted on helpless Iraqis indicts the state even more than do the rampages of Hitler, Mao, or Stalin.

That was typical. Among the excuses for Abu Ghraib's excesses is that low-ranking, untrained soldiers ran it without supervision. The Army implies that while interrogations are rough by nature, Abu Ghraib's staff extrapolated wildly from vague commands. But approval of those rough methods came from on high: "Graner said that Lieutenant Colonel Jordan and Chief Warrant Officer Ed Rivas . . . told him the same thing: 'Whatever you're doing is OK.'" These two regularly patrolled Abu Ghraib and knew "'everything that went on,' Graner said, and 'everything seemed to be fine.'" Nor did this evil originate with the officers. It descended from the very top, though the book doesn't make this point: President Bush has admitted to approving the torture such advisers as Condoleezza Rice and Donald Rumsfeld urged on the Army.

Who Were They?

Who were Abu Ghraib's sadists? Were they Americans like you and I, flummoxed by fate? Were they basically good kids gone bad, or bad kids turned loose? Frighteningly, the answers are "yes," "yes," and "yes." Many of the soldiers sent to Iraq start off idealistic—and ignorant. The nationalism that now passes for patriotism abounds: most are convinced that American culture and government are the world's best. Foreigners who don't embrace both are stupid. That justifies compelling them at gunpoint to accept the Americans overrunning their country. The troops see themselves as "freeing" and "helping" Iraqis; they seem honestly mystified when Iraqis don't welcome that help. Ken Davis, a "road MP [Military Police], a transport man," drives those prisoners lucky enough to merit a trial to and from court. "I'm here to help these people," he says after an attack on his convoy, "and now they're trying to kill me." But such "help" violates the Constitution—and human nature: people always hate the empires and the soldiers conquering them.

To produce an abomination like Abu Ghraib, combine this ignorance and jingoism with the Army's culture of loyalty and unquestioning obedience. Then add the lack of personal morality that increasingly infects our society. *Standard Operating Procedure* portrays the soldiers at Abu Ghraib as hearty partyers, fornicating, blaspheming, lying. The question is never, "Is this right?" but "What's Army regs?" We marvel not that Abu Ghraib festered, but that more mayhem hasn't come to light in the 130 or so countries where the U.S. Army is based.

Standard Operating Procedure has its quirks. It lacks an index, which makes it tough to refresh your memory as to whether an officer mentioned 50 pages ago was a colonel or a captain. Bizarrely, it refers to elected officials by title alone, never by name: George Bush is always "the president," even when first mentioned. Prepare for salty language since the book consists largely of the soldiers' own words. But perhaps the most insidious drawback is the book's novelistic flavor: it is as captivating as fiction, full of twists and turns and characters we come to know well. I caught myself empathizing with the abusers. Realize how seductive the narrative is so you can guard against the idea that everyone in a similar situation would torture.

Dare the biggest neocon or socialist you know to read *Standard Operating Procedure*. Though nothing else persuades him of government's evil, this book should. The suffering U.S. troops have inflicted on helpless Iraqis indicts the state even more than do the rampages of [dictators Adolf] Hitler, Mao [Zedong], or [Joseph] Stalin. We expect atrocities from dictators. But since when have Americans rounded up innocent people by the hundreds, interned them in prison camps, and tortured them?

10

Coercive Interrogation Provides Useful Information

Michael Hayden and Michael B. Mukasey

Michael Hayden was director of the Central Intelligence Agency from 2006–2009. Michael B. Mukasey was attorney general of the United States from 2007 to 2009.

President Barack Obama signed an executive order that limits interrogation techniques to those in the Army Field Manual. Terrorists are now aware of the limits of what government interrogators can do to obtain information from suspects in custody, and they can train to resist these techniques. The goal of coercive interrogation is not to get a confession from the suspect, but information, which can be verified later. Coercive interrogation techniques were used only on a few prisoners who had resisted all other forms of interrogation. The information obtained from these suspects was valuable: it led to the capture of important terrorist leaders and disrupted terrorist plots against the United States and Europe.

The [President Barack] Obama administration has declassified and released opinions of the Justice Department's Office of Legal Counsel (OLC) given in 2005 and earlier that analyze the legality of interrogation techniques authorized for use by the CIA [Central Intelligence Agency]. Those techniques were applied only when expressly permitted by the director, and are described in these opinions in detail, along with their limits and the safeguards applied to them.

Michael Hayden and Michael B. Mukasey, "The President Ties His Own Hands on Terror," *The Wall Street Journal*, April 17, 2009, p. A13. Copyright © 2009 Dow Jones & Company. All rights reserved. Reprinted with permission of *The Wall Street Journal* and the authors.

Limits on Interrogation Techniques

The release of these opinions was unnecessary as a legal matter, and is unsound as a matter of policy. Its effect will be to invite the kind of institutional timidity and fear of recrimination that weakened intelligence gathering in the past, and that we came sorely to regret on Sept. 11, 2001.

Proponents of the release have argued that the techniques have been abandoned and thus there is no point in keeping them secret any longer; that they were in any event ineffective; that their disclosure was somehow legally compelled; and that they cost us more in the coin of world opinion than they were worth. None of these claims survives scrutiny.

Terrorists are now aware of the absolute limit of what the U.S. government could do to extract information from them.

Soon after he was sworn in [January 2009], President Barack Obama signed an executive order that suspended use of these techniques and confined not only the military but all U.S. agencies—including the CIA—to the interrogation limits set in the Army Field Manual. This suspension was accompanied by a commitment to further study the interrogation program, and government personnel were cautioned that they could no longer rely on earlier opinions of the OLC.

Although evidence shows that the Army Field Manual, which is available online, is already used by al Qaeda [terrorist organization responsible for September 11, 2001, attacks] for training purposes, it was certainly the president's right to suspend use of any technique. However, public disclosure of the OLC opinions, and thus of the techniques themselves, assures that terrorists are now aware of the absolute limit of what the U.S. government could do to extract information from them, and can supplement their training accordingly and thus diminish the effectiveness of these techniques as they have the ones in the Army Field Manual.

Moreover, disclosure of the details of the program pre-empts the study of the president's task force and assures that the suspension imposed by the president's executive order is effectively permanent. There would be little point in the president authorizing measures whose nature and precise limits have already been disclosed in detail to those whose resolve we hope to overcome. This conflicts with the sworn promise of the current director of the CIA, Leon Panetta, who testified in aid of securing Senate confirmation that if he thought he needed additional authority to conduct interrogation to get necessary information, he would seek it from the president. By allowing this disclosure, President Obama has tied not only his own hands but also the hands of any future administration faced with the prospect of attack.

Confessions aren't the point. Intelligence is. Interrogation is conducted by using such obvious approaches as asking questions whose correct answers are already known.

Disclosure of the techniques is likely to be met by faux outrage, and is perfectly packaged for media consumption. It will also incur the utter contempt of our enemies. Somehow, it seems unlikely that the people who beheaded [American businessman] Nicholas Berg and [*Wall Street Journal* reporter] Daniel Pearl, and have tortured and slain other American captives, are likely to be shamed into giving up violence by the news that the U.S. will no longer interrupt the sleep cycle of captured terrorists even to help elicit intelligence that could save the lives of its citizens.

An Ignorant View of Interrogations

Which brings us to the next of the justifications for disclosing and thus abandoning these measures: that they don't work anyway, and that those who are subjected to them will simply make up information in order to end their ordeal. This ignorant view of how interrogations are conducted is belied by both experience and common sense. If coercive interrogation had been administered to obtain confessions, one might understand the argument. Khalid Sheikh Mohammed (KSM), who organized the Sept. 11, 2001 attacks, among others, and who has boasted of having beheaded Daniel Pearl, could eventually have felt pressed to provide a false confession. But confessions aren't the point. Intelligence is. Interrogation is conducted by using such obvious approaches as asking questions whose correct answers are already known and only when truthful information is provided proceeding to what may not be known. Moreover, intelligence can be verified, correlated and used to get information from other detainees, and has been; none of this information is used in isolation.

The terrorist Abu Zubaydah (sometimes derided as a low-level operative of questionable reliability, but who was in fact close to KSM and other senior al Qaeda leaders) disclosed some information voluntarily. But he was coerced into disclosing information that led to the capture of Ramzi bin al Shibh, another of the planners of Sept. 11, who in turn disclosed information which—when combined with what was learned from Abu Zubaydah—helped lead to the capture of KSM and other senior terrorists, and the disruption of follow-on plots aimed at both Europe and the U.S. Details of these successes, and the methods used to obtain them, were disclosed repeatedly in more than 30 congressional briefings and hearings beginning in 2002, and open to all members of the Intelligence Committees of both Houses of Congress beginning in September 2006. Any protestation of ignorance of those details, particularly by members of those committees, is pretense.

Interrogation Techniques Are Selectively Used

The techniques themselves were used selectively against only a small number of hard-core prisoners who successfully resisted other forms of interrogation, and then only with the explicit authorization of the director of the CIA. Of the thousands of unlawful combatants captured by the U.S., fewer than 100 were detained and questioned in the CIA program. Of those, fewer than one-third were subjected to any of the techniques discussed in these opinions. As already disclosed by [CIA] Director [Michael] Hayden, as late as 2006, even with the growing success of other intelligence tools, fully half of the government's knowledge about the structure and activities of al Qaeda came from those interrogations.

Nor was there any legal reason compelling such disclosure. To be sure, the American Civil Liberties Union has sued under the Freedom of Information Act to obtain copies of these and other memoranda, but the government until now has successfully resisted such lawsuits. Even when the government disclosed that three members of al Qaeda had been subjected to waterboarding but that the technique was no longer part of the CIA interrogation program, the court sustained the government's argument that the precise details of how it was done, including limits and safeguards, could remain classified against the possibility that some future president may authorize its use. Therefore, notwithstanding the suggestion that disclosure was somehow legally compelled, there was no legal impediment to the Justice Department making the same argument even with respect to any techniques that remained in the CIA program until last January [2009].

A Self-Fulfilling Prophecy

There is something of the self-fulfilling prophecy in the claim that our interrogation of some unlawful combatants beyond the limits set in the Army Field Manual has disgraced us before the world. Such a claim often conflates interrogation with the sadism engaged in by some soldiers at Abu Ghraib [prison in Iraq, where American soldiers abused inmates], an incident that had nothing whatever to do with intelligence gathering.

The limits of the Army Field Manual are entirely appropriate for young soldiers, for the conditions in which they operate, for the detainees they routinely question, and for the kinds of tactically relevant information they pursue. Those limits are not appropriate, however, for more experienced people in controlled circumstances with high-value detainees. Indeed, the Army Field Manual was created with awareness that there was an alternative protocol for high-value detainees.

In addition, there were those who believed that the U.S. deserved what it got on Sept. 11, 2001. Such people, and many who purport to speak for world opinion, were resourceful both before and after the Sept. 11 attacks in crafting reasons to resent America's role as a superpower. Recall also that the first World Trade Center bombing in 1993, the [1998] attacks on our embassies in Kenya and Tanzania, the punctiliously correct trials of defendants in connection with those incidents, and the [2000] bombing of the USS Cole took place long before the advent of CIA interrogations, the invasion of Saddam Hussein's Iraq, or the many other purported grievances asserted over the past eight years.

The techniques themselves were used selectively against only a small number of hard-core prisoners who successfully resisted other forms of interrogation.

The effect of this disclosure on the morale and effectiveness of many in the intelligence community is not hard to predict. Those charged with the responsibility of gathering potentially lifesaving information from unwilling captives are now told essentially that any legal opinion they get as to the lawfulness of their activity is only as durable as political fashion permits. Even with a seemingly binding opinion in hand, which future CIA operations personnel would take the risk? There would be no wink, no nod, no handshake that would convince them that legal guidance is durable. Any president who wants to apply such techniques without such a binding and durable legal opinion had better be prepared to apply them himself.

Beyond that, anyone in government who seeks an opinion from the OLC as to the propriety of any action, or who authors an opinion for the OLC, is on notice henceforth that such a request for advice, and the advice itself, is now more likely than before to be subject after the fact to public and partisan criticism. It is hard to see how that will promote candor either from those who should be encouraged to ask for advice before they act, or from those who must give it.

In his book *The Terror Presidency*, Jack Goldsmith describes the phenomenon we are now experiencing, and its inevitable effect, referring to what he calls "cycles of timidity and aggression" that have weakened intelligence gathering in the past. Politicians pressure the intelligence community to push to the legal limit, and then cast accusations when aggressiveness goes out of style, thereby encouraging risk aversion, and then, as occurred in the wake of 9/11, criticizing the intelligence community for feckless timidity. He calls these cycles "a terrible problem for our national security." Indeed they are, and the precipitous release of these OLC opinions simply makes the problem worse.

11

Other Interrogation Methods Provide More Reliable Information

Ali Soufan

Ali Soufan, a security consultant in the Middle East, is a former investigator for the Federal Bureau of Investigation who was involved in the interrogations of Abu Zubaydah, who is alleged to have been a trusted aide of Osama bin Laden, leader of the terrorist organization, al Qaeda.

Using enhanced interrogation techniques to obtain information from suspects is ineffective and produces unreliable results. A more effective means of interrogation is the Informed Interrogation Approach, which uses the interrogator's knowledge about the suspect to obtain more information. This method is especially effective because detainees feel isolated and frightened, and they crave human contact. The interrogator is someone to whom the suspect can talk. The detainee and interrogator develop a relationship, and the detainee does not want to jeopardize it by refusing to divulge information. Because the interrogator appears to know a great deal about the detainee and uses this information during interrogations, the detainee may think the interrogator knows more than he does, leading the detainee to think that any lies he may tell will be easily caught. Coercive interrogation techniques are not nearly as effective.

Ali Soufan, "Testimony of Ali Soufan before the US Senate Committee on the Judiciary," United States Senate, May 13, 2009.

From my experience—and I speak as someone who has personally interrogated many terrorists and elicited important actionable intelligence—I strongly believe that it is a mistake to use what has become known as the "enhanced interrogation techniques," a position shared by many professional operatives, including the CIA [Central Intelligence Agency] officers who were present at the initial phases of the [terrorist] Abu Zubaydah interrogation.

Ineffective, Slow, Unreliable, and Harmful Techniques

These techniques, from an operational perspective, are ineffective, slow and unreliable, and as a result harmful to our efforts to defeat al Qaeda [terrorist organization responsible for September 11, 2001, attacks]. (This is aside from the important additional considerations that they are un-American and harmful to our reputation and cause.)

My interest in speaking about this issue is not to advocate the prosecution of anyone. People were given misinformation, half-truths, and false claims of successes; and reluctant intelligence officers were given instructions and assurances from higher authorities. Examining a past we cannot change is only worthwhile when it helps guide us towards claiming a better future that is yet within our reach.

And my focus is on the future. I wish to do my part to ensure that we never again use these harmful, slow, ineffective, and unreliable techniques instead of the tried, tested, and successful ones—the ones that are also in sync with our values and moral character. Only by doing this will we defeat the terrorists as effectively and quickly as possible. . . .

The Informed Interrogation Approach

The Informed Interrogation Approach is based on leveraging our knowledge of the detainee's culture and mindset, together with using information we already know about him.

The interrogator knows that there are three primary points of influence on the detainee:

First, there is the fear that the detainee feels as a result of his capture and isolation from his support base. People crave human contact, and this is especially true in some cultures more than others. The interrogator turns this knowledge into an advantage by becoming the one person the detainee can talk to and who listens to what he has to say, and uses this to encourage the detainee to open up.

In addition, acting in a non-threatening way isn't how the detainee is trained to expect a U.S. interrogator to act. This adds to the detainee's confusion and makes him more likely to cooperate.

Second, and connected, there is the need the detainee feels to sustain a position of respect and value to the interrogator. As the interrogator is the one person speaking to and listening to the detainee, a relationship is built—and the detainee doesn't want to jeopardize it. The interrogator capitalizes on this and compels the detainee to give up more information.

The Army Field Manual is not about being nice or soft. It is a knowledge-based approach. It is about outwitting the detainee.

And third, there is the impression the detainee has of the evidence against him. The interrogator has to do his or her homework and become an expert in every detail known to the intelligence community about the detainee. The interrogator then uses that knowledge to impress upon the detainee that everything about him is known and that any lie will be easily caught.

For example, in my first interrogation of the terrorist Abu Zubaydah, who had strong links to al Qaeda's leaders and who knew the details of the 9/11 plot before it happened, I asked him his name. He replied with his alias. I then asked him, "how about if I call you Hani?" That was the name his mother nicknamed him as a child. He looked at me in shock, said "ok," and we started talking.

The Army Field Manual is not about being nice or soft. It is a knowledge-based approach. It is about outwitting the detainee by using a combination of interpersonal, cognitive, and emotional strategies to get the information needed. If done correctly it's an approach that works quickly and effectively because it outwits the detainee using a method that he is not trained, or able, to resist.

This Informed Interrogation Approach is in sharp contrast with the harsh interrogation approach introduced by outside contractors and forced upon CIA officials to use. The harsh technique method doesn't use the knowledge we have of the detainee's history, mindset, vulnerabilities, or culture, and instead tries to subjugate the detainee into submission through humiliation and cruelty. The approach applies a force continuum, each time using harsher and harsher techniques until the detainee submits.

Gaining Compliance vs. Eliciting Cooperation

The idea behind the technique is to force the detainee to see the interrogator as the master who controls his pain. It is an exercise in trying to gain compliance rather than eliciting cooperation. A theoretical application of this technique is a situation where the detainee is stripped naked and told: "Tell us what you know."

There is no way to know whether the detainee is being truthful, or just speaking to either mitigate his discomfort or to deliberately provide false information.

If the detainee doesn't immediately respond by giving information, for example he asks: "what do you want to know?"

the interviewer will reply: "you know," and walk out of the interrogation room. Then the next step on the force continuum is introduced, for example sleep deprivation, and the process will continue until the detainee's will is broken and he automatically gives up all information he is presumed to know. There are many problems with this technique.

Major Problems with Harsh Tactics

A major problem is that it is ineffective. Al Qaeda terrorists are trained to resist torture. As shocking as these techniques are to us, the al Qaeda training prepares them for much worse—the torture they would expect to receive if caught by dictatorships, for example.

This is why, as we see from the recently released Department of Justice memos on interrogation, the contractors had to keep getting authorization to use harsher and harsher methods, until they reached waterboarding and then there was nothing they could do but use that technique again and again. Abu Zubaydah had to be waterboarded 83 times and Khalid Sheikh Mohammed [KSM] 183 times. In a democracy there is a glass ceiling of harsh techniques the interrogator cannot breach, and a detainee can eventually call the interrogator's bluff.

In addition the harsh techniques only serve to reinforce what the detainee has been prepared to expect if captured. This gives him a greater sense of control and predictability about his experience, and strengthens his will to resist.

A second major problem with this technique is that evidence gained from it is unreliable. There is no way to know whether the detainee is being truthful, or just speaking to either mitigate his discomfort or to deliberately provide false information. As the interrogator isn't an expert on the detainee or the subject matter, nor has he spent time going over the details of the case, the interrogator cannot easily know if the detainee is telling the truth. This unfortunately has happened and we have had problems ranging from agents chasing false leads to the disastrous case of Ibn Sheikh al-Libby who gave false information on Iraq, al Qaeda, and WMD [weapons of mass destruction].

Within the first hour of the interrogation, using the Informed Interrogation Approach, we gained important actionable intelligence.

A third major problem with this technique is that it is slow. It takes place over a long period of time, for example preventing the detainee from sleeping for 180 hours as the memos detail, or waterboarding 183 times in the case of KSM. When we have an alleged "ticking timebomb" scenario and need to get information quickly, we can't afford to wait that long. . . .

Immediate, Effective Results

The case of the terrorist Abu Zubaydah is a good example of where the success of the Informed Interrogation Approach can be contrasted with the failure of the harsh technique approach. I have to restrict my remarks to what has been unclassified. (I will note that there is documented evidence supporting everything I will tell you today.)

Immediately after Abu Zubaydah was captured, a fellow FBI [Federal Bureau of Investigation] agent and I were flown to meet him at an undisclosed location. We were both very familiar with Abu Zubaydah and have successfully interrogated al-Qaeda terrorists. We started interrogating him, supported by CIA officials who were stationed at the location, and within the first hour of the interrogation, using the Informed Interrogation Approach, we gained important actionable intelligence.

The information was so important that, as I later learned from open sources, it went to CIA Director George Tenet, who was so impressed that he initially ordered us to be congratulated. That was apparently quickly withdrawn as soon as Mr. Tenet was told that it was FBI agents who were responsible. He then immediately ordered a CIA CTC [Counter Terrorism Center] interrogation team to leave [Washington] DC and head to the location to take over from us.

During his capture Abu Zubaydah had been injured. After seeing the extent of his injuries, the CIA medical team supporting us decided they were not equipped to treat him and we had to take him to a hospital or he would die. At the hospital, we continued our questioning as much as possible, while taking into account his medical condition and the need to know all information he might have on existing threats.

We were once again very successful and elicited information regarding the role of KSM as the mastermind of the 9/11 attacks, and lots of other information that remains classified. (It is important to remember that before this we had no idea of KSM's role in 9/11 or his importance in the al Qaeda leadership structure.) All this happened before the CTC team arrived.

Harsh Techniques Yield No Results

A few days after we started questioning Abu Zubaydah, the CTC interrogation team finally arrived from DC with a contractor who was instructing them on how they should conduct the interrogations, and we were removed. Immediately, on the instructions of the contractor, harsh techniques were introduced, starting with nudity. (The harsher techniques mentioned in the memos were not introduced or even discussed at this point.)

The new techniques did not produce results as Abu Zubaydah shut down and stopped talking. At that time nudity and low-level sleep deprivation (between 24 and 48 hours) was being used. After a few days of getting no information, and after repeated inquiries from DC asking why all of sudden no information was being transmitted (when before there had been a steady stream), we again were given control of the interrogation.

We then returned to using the Informed Interrogation Approach. Within a few hours, Abu Zubaydah again started talking and gave us important actionable intelligence.

This included the details of Jose Padilla, the so-called "dirty bomber." To remind you of how important this information was viewed at the time, the then-Attorney General, John Ashcroft, held a press conference from Moscow to discuss the news. Other important actionable intelligence was also gained that remains classified.

After a few days, the contractor attempted to once again try his untested theory and he started reimplementing the harsh techniques. He moved this time further along the force continuum, introducing loud noise and then temperature manipulation.

Protests Are Overruled

Throughout this time, my fellow FBI agent and I, along with a top CIA interrogator who was working with us, protested, but we were overruled. I should also note that another colleague, an operational psychologist for the CIA, had left the location because he objected to what was being done.

Again, however, the technique wasn't working and Abu Zubaydah wasn't revealing any information, so we were once again brought back in to interrogate him. We found it harder to reengage him this time, because of how the techniques had affected him, but eventually, we succeeded, and he re-engaged again.

Once again the contractor insisted on stepping up the notches of his experiment, and this time he requested the authorization to place Abu Zubaydah in a confinement box, as the next stage in the force continuum. While everything I saw to this point [was] nowhere near the severity later listed in the memos, the evolution of the contractor's theory, along with what I had seen till then, struck me as "borderline torture."

As the Department of Justice IG [Inspector General] report released last year [2008] states, I protested to my superiors in the FBI and refused to be a part of what was happening. The Director of the FBI, Robert Mueller, a man I deeply respect, agreed, passing the message that "we don't do that," and I was pulled out. . . .

It was a mistake to abandon [the Informed Interrogation Approach] in favor of harsh interrogation methods that are harmful, shameful, slower, unreliable, ineffective, and play directly into the enemy's handbook.

One of the Worst and Most Harmful Decisions

In summary, the Informed Interrogation Approach outlined in the Army Field Manual is the most effective, reliable, and speedy approach we have for interrogating terrorists. It is legal and has worked time and again.

It was a mistake to abandon it in favor of harsh interrogation methods that are harmful, shameful, slower, unreliable, ineffective, and play directly into the enemy's handbook. It was a mistake to abandon an approach that was working and naively replace it with an untested method. It was a mistake to abandon an approach that is based on the cumulative wisdom and successful tradition of our military, intelligence, and law enforcement community, in favor of techniques advocated by contractors with no relevant experience.

The mistake was so costly precisely because the situation was, and remains, too risky to allow someone to experiment with amateurish, Hollywood style interrogation methods— that in reality taint sources, risk outcomes, ignore the end game, and diminish our moral high ground in a battle that is impossible to win without first capturing the hearts and minds around the world. It was one of the worst and most harmful decisions made in our efforts against al Qaeda.

12

Torture Raises Questions About Democratic Values

Frida Ghitis

Frida Ghitis is a reporter for the Miami Herald.

Many debates on torture have focused on whether it works. If the assumption is made that torture does work, the debate becomes far more complex: Is saving human lives (using information obtained through torture) more valuable than preserving democratic principles? Many people have given their lives fighting to protect democracy. America, and all democracies, must decide the value of human life, morality, and the rule of law.

Americans engaged in the debate about torture are taking part in one of the most important discussions a society can have. If honestly faced, the arguments on all sides may reveal the character and priorities of the country: What matters more, human rights or human life; the rule of law or the security of a nation? So far, however, an indispensable piece for a truly useful debate has remained outside the conversation.

Until now, the discussion has gone something like this: Opponents of torture say torture simply doesn't work, producing only false confessions. Proponents of harsh interrogation say the questionable methods are indisputably required to secure the country. This argument fails to scratch the surface. It takes us nowhere.

A Critically Important Decision

If it is true that torture produces only unreliable information then there is nothing to discuss. There is no moral dilemma. If, on the other hand, torture does elicit the kind of information that can prevent terrorist attacks and save human lives, then Americans must make a truly excruciating, but critically important decision.

Forget for a moment that disgraced former Vice President Dick Cheney is the man calling for the release of evidence about whether or not the euphemistically labeled "enhanced interrogation techniques" worked. The fact that Cheney, one of the least popular men in America, says the memos should come out does not mean they should remain secret. Cheney mistakenly believes that once we are offered proof that torture saved lives the discussion will end. He is wrong about that. If we all agree that torture works, that's when the debate only begins.

Picture Daniel Pearl—many now call him "Danny," as if he had become a personal friend. The American reporter captured by terrorists in Pakistan in 2002 was slowly decapitated by Khalid Sheik Mohammed while a video camera recorded the horror for the world to see.

Mohammed, who was "water boarded" by U.S. interrogators, proudly proclaimed he was the man brandishing the knife that cut across Pearl's throat.

What if torture could have produced a piece of information to prevent the murder? What if torture could have prevented 9/11 [2001] and allowed thousands of children, wives, parents and friends to continue enjoying the company and attention of their parents, spouses and loved ones killed in the attacks?

Democracy and the Value of a Human Life

It goes without saying that human life is precious. Is it, however, more valuable than anything else? Is it more valuable than the principles upon which a democracy is founded? Anyone who claims these are easy questions is not serious about this discussion.

The United States is not the first country to face this wrenching moral dilemma. After decades of suicide bombings and other terrorist attacks, Israelis have wrestled with this question for years.

Is protecting democracy more important than protecting life? Ask the people who have given their lives fighting for democracy.

The Israeli Supreme Court ruled in 1999 that torture is, in fact, illegal, famously declaring that "a democracy must fight with one hand tied behind its back." Writing in the *Harvard Law Review* in 2002, then-president of the court Aharon Barak argued that, "judges in modern democracies are responsible for protecting democracy both from terrorism and from the means the state wants to use to fight terrorism." Democracy itself, he explained, is under attack not just from terrorists but also from the very methods that can prove effective for fighting terrorism.

What Price Will We Pay for Democracy?

Is protecting democracy more important than protecting life? Ask the people who have given their lives fighting for democracy. There are less philosophical arguments against torture, such as the ones President Barack Obama and others have made. America's standing in the world diminishes when people know it engages in torture and this hurts the fight against terrorists and other enemies.

In addition, the prospect of torture in captivity makes enemy fighters less likely to surrender.

Those points, however well taken, go back to the less-profound question of whether or not torture ultimately works.

The necessary conversation, not just for America but for all democracies—nations that value human life, morality and the rule of law—is what price we are willing to pay to protect those sacrosanct principles?

No debate will tell us more about who we are and who we want to be.

13

Torture Is Permissible in a Democracy

Mirko Bagaric and Julie Clarke

Mirko Bagaric is a law professor at Deakin University in Melbourne, Australia. Julie Clarke is a lecturer in law at Deakin University. Editors note: Additions in [brackets] and subheads are not a part of the original text.

Life-saving torture and democracy can coexist side by side. Most Americans would support the use of torture to thwart a terrorist attack and save lives. Governments often sacrifice the interests of individuals for the greater good. The right to life of thousands of potential victims far outweighs the rights of a few terrorists. Several democratic countries have used torture over the years, and none has sunk into barbarism.

[A] supposed downside of torture is that it is antidemocratic or will corrupt democracy. Some critics [including Anne O'Rourke et al.] have even put it as high as that it will have a "devastating effect" on democracy. This is a confusing argument because its main premise is not spelled out. Democracy is a complex and ill-defined notion. If it means majoritarianism, as many believe to be the case, then a lawfully elected government can obviously through its normal political process legalize torture. If the normal law-making process is observed, then life-saving torture and democracy sit harmoniously.

Mirko Bagaric and Julie Clarke, *Torture: When the Unthinkable Is Morally Permissible.* Albany, NY: State University of New York Press, 2007, pp. 63–67. Copyright © 2007 State University of New York. Reproduced by permission of the State University of New York Press.

Most Support Torture to Prevent an Attack

It is certainly not inconceivable that a robust and free democracy would permit life-saving torture. The latest [2005] *Newsweek* poll on the subject shows that:

> 44 percent of the public thinks torture is often or sometimes justified as a way to obtain important information, while 51 percent say it is rarely or never justified. A clear majority—58 percent—would support torture to thwart a terrorist attack, but asked if they would still support torture if that made it more likely enemies would use it against Americans, 57 percent said no. Some 73 percent agree that America's image abroad has been hurt by the torture allegations.

These findings are confirmed by a more wide-ranging poll by AP-Ipsos reported in December 2005. It showed that in addition to Americans, a majority of people in Britain, France, and South Korea also approved of torturing terrorism suspects in rare instances. In Canada, Mexico, and Germany, the community is split on whether torture is justified in any circumstances. Of the nine countries surveyed, only majorities in Spain and Italy opposed torture in all circumstances.

When forced to choose between two evils, we always elect for the lesser evil. Notions of individual rights go missing in the process.

Societies, When Pressed, Always Choose the Lesser Evil

Moreover, ... when (democratic) societies have their backs to the wall and they are forced to make difficult choices, they invariably go down the path of least harm. [There are] several examples of the preparedness of governments to sacrifice the interests of individuals for the greater good, such as forcing soldiers to go to war and the like. The principle behind such decisions has not been challenged by the critics. But for illustrative purposes we add to the catalogue of situations that make it clear that, when forced to choose between two evils, we always elect for the lesser evil. Notions of individual rights go missing in the process.

The English Court of Appeals in the case of *Re A (Children)* in 2000 held that it was permissible to kill one conjoined twin in order to improve the chances that the other would live. This was despite the fact that there was no guarantee that the stronger twin would survive the operation. Why did the Court make this decision? Pressed to make a choice between important conflicting rights, the judge resolved the matter "by choosing the lesser of the two evils and so finding the least detrimental alternative."

For another "real life" example of what we do in extreme cases, refer to the Zeebrugge disaster in 1987 [a British ferry capsized outside the Belgian port of Zeebrugge killing 193 people]. Dozens of people were in the water and in danger of drowning. They were near the foot of a rope ladder, but their route to safety was blocked for at least ten minutes by a young man who was petrified by cold or fear (or both) and was unable to move. The corporal gave instructions to push him off the ladder. He was never seen again. What if instead of blocking the ladder the young man refused to provide the pin number to release the ladder? There is not too much doubt that he would have been subjected to some "physical persuasion."

Forced to Testify

Continuing with the real-life theme (to finally bury the claim that the examples we cite belong in the realms of fiction), . . . most countries have laws that compel witnesses to give evidence in court. This is even if they do not wish to and in fact have strong reasons for not giving evidence. Yet we compel them to do so, no matter what level of mental anguish this causes them and the level of danger that this places them in. A recent illustration involves twenty-seven-year-old Melbourne [Australia] lawyer Zarah Garde-Williams. She was found guilty of contempt of court for refusing to testify against two "gangsters" who had murdered her boyfriend. The murders were in the context of unprecedented underworld killings in Melbourne resulting in the execution-style killings of more than 20 "gangland" figures over several years. During questions by the judge about her involvement with the victim (her former boyfriend), she wept in the witness box and responded that she was "unable to answer questions due to fear for [her] safety." One of the accused threatened her and she said that she believed she would get her "head blown off" if she gave evidence. She applied to enter a police witness protection program but this was rejected. Still, the fact that Ms. Garde-Williams thought she would be killed if she gave evidence and was obviously traumatized about the prospect of giving evidence did not find much favor with the judge. In finding her guilty of contempt for refusing to answer the questions, Justice Harper stated that her fear was no excuse for not giving evidence and that if other witnesses in murder trials also refused to testify, "no system of justice could survive."

Thus, here we have a situation where the criminal justice system is using the threat of imprisonment to coerce information from a traumatized innocent individual who has reasonable grounds for believing that she would be killed if she obeyed the law. Given a choice between this ordeal and a dose of physical persuasion there would be no doubt that many people would prefer the former. As a community we often treat individuals very harshly when the common good is at stake. It is an undeniable fact. Yet democracy remains intact.

An Absence of Argument

And as a side issue, note the absence of the arguments that are used against our life-saving torture proposal in the context of compelled witness disclosure. In this context, there are no utterances along the lines that we should not force witnesses to give evidence because we can never be sure that the witness has the evidence, the witness might lie, and so on. These arguments resonate very strongly with the torture critics but are muted in the context of other institutionalized practices that can have a crushing impact on individuals. These arguments are in reality just as futile in the context of torture.

The history of humankind shows that when societies are threatened they prioritize the common good over individual interests.

Some critics have sought to pad out the notion of democracy slightly by suggesting that it is built on the foundation of respect for individuals and human rights and that torture runs counter to this. This in essence is the dehumanizing point repeated under a different banner. If democracy does entail respect for individuals and human rights, then surely each individual counts equally in this process, including that of potential victims.

Even if we move from strictly majoritarianism accounts of democracy to more expansive and sophisticated accounts of the nature of democracy, which contend that democracy is a substantive rather than a procedural concept, there seems no scope for labelling the institutionalization of life-saving torture as a threat to democracy. For example, the democratic ideal adopted by [philosopher] Samuel Freeman provides that the only political and social institutions that are justifiable by Democratic sovereignty are those that reflect the interests common to all people. It can hardly be doubted that the highest-order interest shared by at least most people is the right to life.

Moreover, as is noted by [British newspaper editor Alasdair] Palmer, countries such as France, Britain, and Israel have all used torture widely over the past fifty years and "none has sunk into barbarism, or ceased to be a law-governed democracy."

If the critics want to persuasively advance the democracy counter, they need to spell out the key indicia of such a concept and how it is incompatible with going down the path of the lesser evil. The critics have much work to do on this front.

The Antidemocratic Argument Is Wrong

The antidemocratic criticism is factually wrong. The history of humankind shows that when societies are threatened they prioritize the common good over individual interests. . . . The critics have not referred to a single counterexample to our claim.

Organizations to Contact

The editors have compiled the following list of organizations concerned with the issues debated in this book. The descriptions are derived from materials provided by the organizations. All have publications or information available for interested readers. The list was compiled on the date of publication of the present volume; names, addresses, and phone numbers may change. Be aware that many organizations take several weeks or longer to respond to inquiries, so allow as much time as possible.

Action by Christians Against Torture (ACAT)
8 Southfield, Saltash, Cornwall   PL12 4LX
   United Kingdom
01752 843417
e-mail: uk.acat@googlemail.com
Web site: www.acatuk.org.uk

Action by Christians Against Torture was formed, with the active support of Amnesty International, to work for the abolition of torture worldwide by increasing awareness among Christians of the widespread use of torture. As part of this work, ACAT seeks information on specific examples of torture, advocates with governments, keeps abreast of legislation, and supports victims of torture. ACAT publishes a bimonthly newsletter on torture, available on its Web site.

American Civil Liberties Union (ACLU)
125 Broad St., 18th Floor, New York, NY   10004
(212) 549-2500 • fax: (212) 549-2646
Web site: www.aclu.org

The ACLU is a national organization that works to defend Americans' civil rights as guaranteed by the U.S. Constitution. It provides legal defense, research, and education. The ACLU's numerous publications include "In Defense of Freedom in a

Time of Crisis"; "Bigger Monster, Weaker Chains: The Growth
of an American Surveillance Society"; and "Civil Liberties After 9-11: The ACLU Defends Freedom."

Amnesty International USA

5 Penn Plaza, New York, NY   10001
(212) 807-8400 • fax: (212) 627-1451
e-mail: aimember@aiusa.org
Web site: www.amnestyusa.org

Amnesty International is a grassroots organization whose mission is to protect people from human rights violations. It believes that in the "war on terror," the U.S. government has
subjected people who have not been charged with or convicted of a crime to torture and other cruel, inhuman, and degrading treatment, and that these practices are immoral and
illegal. Amnesty International undertakes research and action
to prevent and end human rights abuses. Its Web site contains
information and briefs about torture and countering terrorism with justice.

Brookings Institution

1775 Massachusetts Ave. NW, Washington, DC   20036
(202) 797-6000 • fax: (202) 797-6004
e-mail: brookinfo@brook.edu
Web site: www.brookings.edu

The Brookings Institution, founded in 1927, is a think tank
that conducts research and education in foreign policy, eco-
nomics, government, and the social sciences. In 2001, it began
America's Response to Terrorism, a project that provides briefings and analysis to the public and which is featured on the
institution's Web site. Its Web site includes transcripts from
congressional testimony, interviews, and white papers about
rendition, interrogations, and torture. Among its publications
are a series of white papers, including "Counterterrorism and
American Statutory Law," the quarterly *Brookings Review*, and
periodic *Policy Briefs*.

Center for Defense Information

1779 Massachusetts Ave. NW, Suite 615
Washington, DC   20036
(202) 332-0600 • fax: (202) 462-4559
e-mail: info@cdi.org
Web site: www.cdi.org

The Center for Defense Information is a non-partisan, non-profit organization that researches all aspects of global security. It seeks to educate the public and policy makers about issues such as security strategies and terrorism. It publishes the monthly publication *Defense Monitor* and has published the book *Imperial America: A Double-Barreled Attack on American War Policy*. Its Web site includes copies of treaties and conventions against torture as well as news articles about torture.

Center for Justice & Accountability (CJA)

870 Market St., Suite 688, San Francisco, CA   94102
(415) 544-0444 • fax: (415) 544-0456
e-mail: center4justice@cja.org
Web site: www.cja.org

The Center for Justice & Accountability is an international human rights organization dedicated to ending torture and other severe human rights abuses around the world. CJA uses litigation to hold perpetrators individually accountable for human rights abuses, develop human rights law, and advance the rule of law in countries making the transition from periods of abuse. CJA's Web site provides information for survivors, information about its cases, various publications, and links to other human rights organizations concerned with torture.

Center for Victims of Torture (CVT)

1875 I St. NW, 5th Floor, Washington, DC   20006
(202) 857-3284 • fax: (202) 429-9574
e-mail: cvt@cvt.org
Web site: www.cvt.org

The Center for Victims of Torture was founded to stop government-sponsored torture and to heal the wounds that torture inflicts on individuals, their families, and communities. CVT does this by providing services directly to torture survivors; training health, education, and human services professionals who work with torture survivors; conducting research on the effects of torture and treatment methods; and advocating for public policy initiatives to help survivors and put an end to torture worldwide. CVT's Web site offers journal articles and a useful bibliography on the subject of torture.

Central Intelligence Agency (CIA)
Office of Public Affairs, Washington, DC 20505
(703) 482-0623 • fax: (703) 482-1739
Web site: www.cia.gov

The CIA was created in 1947 by President Harry S. Truman and is responsible for collecting—openly and secretly—information about foreign governments, corporations, and individuals who may pose a threat to the safety of the United States. The CIA also is charged with analyzing and reporting its findings to various agencies of the government. Publications, including *Factbook on Intelligence*, are available on its Web site.

Heritage Foundation
214 Massachusetts Ave. NE, Washington, DC 20002
(202) 546-4400 • fax: (202) 546-0904
e-mail: info@heritage.org
Web site: www.heritage.org

The Heritage Foundation is a conservative public policy research institute dedicated to free-market principles, individual liberty, and limited government. Its resident scholars publish position papers on a wide range of issues in its *Backgrounder* series and in its quarterly journal *Policy Review*. Available on its Web site are recent articles, including "Set the Record Straight: Publish All Key Memos on CIA Interrogations"; "The Torture Test"; and "The Rule of Pain." It also has archived a symposium it sponsored: *24 and America's Image in Fighting Terrorism: Fact, Fiction, or Does It Matter?*

Human Rights First

333 Seventh Ave., 13th Floor, New York, NY   10001-5108
(212) 845-5200 • fax: (212) 845-5299
e-mail: feedback@humanrightsfirst.org
Web site: www.humanrightsfirst.org

Human Rights First was originally founded as the Lawyers Committee for International Human Rights. Its mission is to protect people at risk, including victims of torture and crimes against humanity. It advocates for changes in government and international policies, seeks justice through the courts, and raises awareness and understanding through the media. Its Web site contains links to numerous publications, many related to torture and human rights abuses, including "Behind the Wire" and "Tortured Justice: Using Coerced Evidence to Prosecute Terrorist Suspects."

Human Rights Watch (HRW)

1630 Connecticut Ave. NE, Suite 500, Washington, DC   20009
(202) 612-4321 • fax: (202) 612-4333
e-mail: hrwdc@hrw.org
Web site: www.hrw.org

Human Rights Watch conducts fact-finding investigations into human rights abuses and publishes those findings in dozens of books and reports. HRW also meets with government officials to urge changes in policy and practice and provides up-to-the-minute information about conflicts while they are under way. The organization's Web site contains numerous publications about torture around the world, including news articles, legislative statements, and commentary.

Rand Corporation

1776 Main St., PO Box 2138, Santa Monica, CA   90407-2138
(310) 393-0411 • fax: (310) 393-4818
Web site: www.rand.org

The Rand Corporation is an independent nonprofit organization engaged in research on national security issues and the public welfare. It conducts its work with support from federal, state, and local governments and from foundations and other philanthropic sources. Its publications include the commentary "The Torture Debate: Redux," and the periodical *Rand Review*, which features articles about terrorism and counterterrorism efforts.

United Nations Office of the High Commissioner for Human Rights (OHCHR)

Palais Wilson, 52 rue des Pâquis, Geneva   CH-1201
  Switzerland
+41 22 917 90 00
e-mail: InfoDesk@ohchr.org
Web site: www.ohchr.org

The mission of the United Nations' OHCHR is to work for the protection of all human rights for all people, to help empower people to realize their rights, and to assist those responsible for upholding such rights in ensuring that they are implemented. To carry out this mission, the OHCHR works with governments, legislatures, courts, national institutions, and the United Nations system. The OHCHR Web site is a source of news and events, fact sheets, and other reference materials about torture. The organization's published fact sheets include "The International Bill of Rights," "Combating Torture," and "Torture Under International Law."

Bibliography

Books

Mirko Bagaric and Julie Clarke	*Torture: When the Unthinkable Is Morally Permissible.* Albany, NY: State University of New York Press, 2007.
Bob Brecher	*Torture and the Ticking Bomb.* Malden, MA: Blackwell, 2007.
David Cole, ed.	*The Torture Memos: Rationalizing the Unthinkable.* New York: New Press, 2009.
Laura L. Finley	*The Torture and Prisoner Abuse Debate.* Westport, CT: Greenwood Press, 2008.
Yuval Ginbar	*Why Not Torture Terrorists? Moral, Practical, and Legal Aspects of the "Ticking Bomb" Justification for Torture.* New York: Oxford University Press, 2010.
Karen J. Greenberg, ed.	*The Torture Debate in America.* New York: Cambridge University Press, 2006.
Stephen Grey	*Ghost Plane: The True Story of the CIA Torture Program.* New York: St. Martin's Press, 2006.
Thomas C. Hilde, ed.	*On Torture.* Baltimore, MD: Johns Hopkins University, 2008.

Joseph Margulies *Guantánamo and the Abuse of Presidential Power.* New York: Simon and Schuster, 2006.

Jane Mayer *Dark Side: The Inside Story of How the War on Terror Turned into a War on American Ideals.* New York: Doubleday, 2008.

Alfred C. McCoy *A Question of Torture: CIA Interrogation, from the Cold War to the War on Terror.* New York: Metropolitan/Owl Book/Henry Holt, 2006.

Tara McKelvey *Monstering: Inside America's Policy of Secret Interrogations and Torture in the Terror War.* New York: Carroll & Graf, 2007.

Barbara J. Olshansky *Democracy Detained: Secret, Unconstitutional Practices in the U.S. War on Terror.* New York: Seven Stories Press, 2007.

Michael Otterman *American Torture: From the Cold War to Abu Ghraib and Beyond.* Carlton, Victoria, Australia: Melbourne University Press, 2007.

Charles E. Pederson *Torture.* Yankton, SD: Erickson Press, 2009.

Darius Rejali *Torture and Democracy.* Princeton, NJ: Princeton University Press, 2007.

David Rodin, ed. *War, Torture, and Terrorism: Ethics and War in the 21st Century.* Malden, MA: Blackwell, 2007.

Phillippe Sands | *Torture Team: Rumsfeld's Memo and the Betrayal of American Values.* New York: Palgrave Macmillan, 2008.

William F. Schulz, ed. | *The Phenomenon of Torture: Readings and Commentary.* Philadelphia: University of Pennsylvania Press, 2007.

A.C. Thompson and Trevor Paglen | *Torture Taxi: On the Trail of the CIA's Rendition Flights.* Hoboken, NJ: Melville House, 2006.

Jeremy Wisnewski and R.D. Emerick | *The Ethics of Torture.* New York: Continuum, 2009.

Jessica Wolfendale | *Torture and the Military Profession.* New York: Palgrave Macmillan, 2007.

John Yoo | *War by Other Means: An Insider's Account of the War on Terror.* New York: Atlantic Monthly Press, 2006.

Periodicals

Jonathan Alter | "Cheney's Tortured Logic," *Newsweek,* September 14, 2009.

George M. Anderson | "Healing Torture's Wounds: One Doctor's Fight for the Survivors," *America,* April 21, 2008.

Robert Baer | "Dumb Intelligence," *Time,* May 4, 2009.

Peter Bergen — "The Body Snatchers: Inside the CIA's Extraordinary Rendition Program," *Mother Jones*, March–April 2008.

David Cole — "Truth and Consequences: The Case for a Commission on Torture," *America*, August 3, 2009.

Matthew D'Ancona — "The Spooks Are Squirming," *Spectator*, August 15, 2009.

Economist — "Is Torture Ever Justified?" September 20, 2007.

Joseph Finder — "The C.I.A. in Double Jeopardy," *New York Times*, August 30, 2009.

Philip Hensher — "Hollywood Is Helping Us Learn to Love Torture," *Independent* [UK], June 26, 2007.

Bob Herbert — "Who Are We?" *New York Times*, June 23, 2009.

Michael Isikoff — "We Could Have Done This the Right Way," *Newsweek*, May 4, 2009.

Michael Isikoff and Evan Thomas — "The Lawyer and the Caterpillar," *Newsweek*, April 27, 2009.

Fred Kaplan — "Send Him Back to the Bunker!" *Slate*, May 21, 2009.

Joe Klein — "High Crimes," *Time*, January 19, 2009.

Dahlia Lithwick — "Have We Softened Up on Torture?" *Newsweek*, May 4, 2009.

Jane Mayer "Whatever It Takes: The Politics of the Man Behind '24'," *New Yorker*, February 19, 2007.

Andrew C. McCarthy "The Myth of Bush's Torture Regime," *National Review*, December 29, 2008.

Andrew C. McCarthy "Torture Is a State of Mind," *National Review*, May 25, 2009.

Mary Ellen O'Connell "No Excuses: Our Obligations to Prosecute Human Rights Violations," *America*, August 3, 2009.

Progressive "Torturers in the White House," June 2008.

Progressive "No Impunity," June 2009.

Philippe Sands "The Green Light," *Vanity Fair*, May 2008.

Luiza Ch. Savage "Tortured Logic," *Maclean's*, July 28, 2008.

Scott Shane and Mark Mazzetti "Records Show Strict Rules for CIA Interrogations," *New York Times*, August 26, 2009.

Justine Sharrock "First, Do No Harm: The Rules Are Crystal Clear: Doctors Can't Take Part in Torture," *Mother Jones*, July–August 2009.

Michael Slackman "What's Wrong with Torturing an al Qaeda Higher-Up?" *New York Times*, May 16, 2004.

Ali Soufan   "What Torture Never Told Us," *New York Times*, September 6, 2009.

Mary Zeiss Stange "Witch Hunts and Torture," *USA Today*, June 29, 2009.

Stuart Taylor Jr.   "The Truth About Torture," *Newsweek*, July 21, 2008.

Marc Thiessen   "The *Post* and Abu Zubaydah," *National Review Online*, March 29, 2009.

Jaime J. Weinman "Should Torturers Pay Royalties?" *Maclean's*, August 4, 2008.

Paul Wells   "Obama's Torture Problem Is Only Just Beginning," *Maclean's*, April 6, 2009.

Brian Zabcik   "Without a Trace: Torture Persists Because Interrogators Learned How to Cover Their Tracks with Techniques That Don't Leave Any Marks," *American Lawyer*, May 2008.

Index